Preface

The field of web technologies has grown exponentially, transforming how businesses and individuals interact with the digital world. As the internet continues to evolve, mastering web technologies has become a crucial skill for computer science professionals. This book, IGNOU MCS - 220 Web Technologies: Previous Years Unsolved Papers, is designed to assist students in their journey to becoming proficient in web development and technologies. By focusing on past unsolved question papers, the book serves as an essential resource for students enrolled in the MCS-220 course at Indira Gandhi National Open University (IGNOU).

The MCS-220 course on Web Technologies is an integral part of the Master of Computer Applications (MCA) curriculum, aimed at providing students with the theoretical knowledge and practical skills needed to develop web applications and services. This course covers a wide array of topics, including HTML, CSS, JavaScript, web programming, client-server architecture, and database connectivity, among others. With web technologies at the forefront of modern computing, gaining mastery in these areas is vital for both academic success and professional growth.

This book brings together a collection of unsolved question papers from previous years, offering students the opportunity to practice and apply their knowledge in a structured and focused manner. The aim of this book is to provide students with a hands-on approach to learning, allowing them to engage with real-world questions that have been part of the examination process. By working through these papers, students can better understand the exam pattern, improve their problem-solving skills, and boost their confidence in tackling complex questions.

The significance of solving previous years' question papers cannot be overstated. Exams often tend to follow certain patterns, and practicing these papers allows students to get familiar with the types of questions they are likely to encounter in their actual exams. This book serves as a critical tool for exam preparation by offering unsolved papers that encourage students to test their understanding and think critically about the subject matter.

The practice of working through unsolved questions also helps students identify areas where they may need further study or clarification. In web technologies, where both conceptual understanding and practical application are crucial, this kind of targeted practice is invaluable. By solving these papers, students not only reinforce their theoretical knowledge but also gain the practical skills necessary to excel in web development projects.

Table of Contents

MCS-220

Master Of Computer Applications (MCA)
Chapter 1: Term-End Examination, December, 2021
MCS-220: Web Technologies

Time: 3 Hours
Maximum Marks: 100
Note:(i) Question No. 1 is compulsory.
(ii) Attempt any three questions from therest.

1. (a) What is design pattern? What are the advantages of using patterns? Explain UMLdiagram of Factory Design Pattern. 10

(b) What is Servlet Programming? Briefly explain servlet life cycle. Also write a servlet which displays "welcome to web programming." 10

(c) What is JSP? What are JSP directives? Explain the use of any two JSP directives with the help of a program. 10

(d) Explain process of setting up database using Hibernate. 10

2. (a) Explain process of creating records using Spring Boot and Hibernate. 10

(b) Explain how testing of custom login form can be performed with the help of anexample. 10

3. (a) Explain issues and challenges of web security. 10

(b) What is Spring Boot DevTools? Briefly explain its features. 10

4. (a) Briefly explain Crud Repository of Spring Boot. 10

(b) Explain Spring MVC configuration process. 10

5. Write short notes on the following: 5 each

(a) JSP implicit objects

(b) Role based login

(c) Session management

(d) J2EE Architecture

MCS-220

Master Of Computer Applications (MCA)
Chapter 2: Term-End Examination, June, 2022
MCS-220: Web Technologies

Time: 3 hours
Maximum Marks: 100

Note: Question no. 1 is compulsory and consists of 40 marks.
Attempt any three questions from the rest.

1. (a) What is J2EE? Briefly explain J2EE architecture. (10 Marks)

(b) Explain servlet architecture. Also briefly explain the use of servlet with the help of an example. (10 Marks)

(c) Explain JSP scripting elements with the help of a program. (10 Marks)

(d) What is Spring Boot? Briefly explain Spring Boot application properties. (10 Marks)

2. (a) What is a design pattern? Explain the advantages of using a design pattern in enterprise applications development, with the help of an example. (10 Marks)

(b) Explain Hibernate configuration with annotations. (10 Marks)

3. (a) Explain Spring MVC framework with the help of a suitable diagram. (10 Marks)

(b) Explain the working and flow of Struts 2. (10 Marks)

4. (a) Explain the steps of database connection using JSP and JDBC, with the help of a program. (10 Marks)

(b) Explain the use of load( ) and get( ) methods of Hibernate session, with the help of an example. (10 Marks)

5. Write short notes on the following: (4×5=20 Marks)

(a) Java Cryptography Architecture (JCA)

(b) JSP Standard Tag Library (JSTL)

(c) JSP Life Cycle

(d) Factory Design Pattern

MCS-220

Master Of Computer Applications (MCA)
Chapter 3: Term-End Examination, December, 2022
MCS-220: Web Technologies

Time: 3 hours
Maximum Marks: 100

Note: Question no. 1 is compulsory and consists of 40 marks. Attempt any three questions from the rest.

1. (a) What is a web application? Explain the use of a web server for the development of web applications. Also, describe the differences between a web server and a web container. (10 Marks)

(b) What is a design pattern? Explain the use of the Singleton design pattern with the help of an example. (10 Marks)

(c) What is a Servlet? Explain the use of the HTTP protocol in servlet programming. Explain the use of GET and POST methods with the help of examples. (10 Marks)

(d) What is Struts 2? Explain the core components of Struts 2. (10 Marks)

2. (a) What are JSP implicit objects? Explain the use of any four implicit objects. (10 Marks)

(b) Explain the use of the Authorize Tag for providing view layer security, with the help of program code. (10 Marks)

3. (a) What is Session Management? Write a servlet program to demonstrate the use of HttpSession and its methods setAttribute and getAttribute. (10 Marks)

(b) Explain how Java Secure Socket Extension (JSSE) is used in web security. (10 Marks)

4. (a) Explain core container and its components in the Spring Framework. (10 Marks)

(b) Explain how CRUD is mapped to SQL statements, with examples. (10 Marks)

5. (a) What is Role-based Login? Explain how a user's access can be restricted using Role-based Login. (10 Marks)

(b) Write short notes on the following: (10 Marks)

(i) Servlet Collaboration
(ii) JSP Life Cycle

Master Of Computer Applications (MCA)
Chapter 4: Term-End Examination, June, 2023
MCS-220: Web Technologies

Time: 3 Hours
Maximum Marks: 100

Note:
(i) Question no. 1 is compulsory.
(ii) Attempt any three questions from the rest.

1. (a) Differentiate between web server and web container. Give an example for each. (5 Marks)

(b) Compare GenericServlet with HttpServlet. (5 Marks)

(c) What is session management? Explain how cookies can be used for session management. (5 Marks)

(d) Write a JSP program using scriptlets that adds numbers from 1 to 10 and prints the results. Support your code with suitable comments. (5 Marks)

(e) What is a ValueStack in Struts? How is ValueStack related to OGNL (Object Graph Navigation Language)? (5 Marks)

(f) Differentiate between Spring and Hibernate. (5 Marks)

(g) What is Dependency Injection in the Spring framework? Name the ways through which Dependency Injection can be performed. (5 Marks)

(h) What is Bootstrap? Briefly discuss the factors that make Bootstrap a popular choice for web application development. (5 Marks)

2. (a) What is Spring Boot? Write the steps to deploy a Spring Boot web application as JAR and WAR files. (10 Marks)

(b) What is Hibernate Query Language (HQL)? How does HQL differ from SQL? Write HQL queries for Select, Update, Delete, and Insert (make suitable assumptions). (10 Marks)

3. (a) Briefly discuss the term "Spring Data Repository." Also, explain the CrudRepository, Paging and Sorting Repository, and JpaRepository interfaces of Spring Data Repository. (10 Marks)

(b) Explain the following: (10 Marks)
(i) Java Cryptography Architecture (JCA)
(ii) Java Secure Socket Extension (JSSE)

4. (a) What is Spring Security? Discuss the terms "Authentication" and "Authorization" in the context of Spring Security. Also, mention methods for both. (10 Marks)

(b) Why is login form customization required in an application? Explain the customized login form configuration with a simple code. Also, discuss loginPage() and loginProcessingUrl() in Spring Boot Security Configuration. (10 Marks)

5. Write short notes on the following: (5×4=20 Marks)

(i) Servlet Architecture
(ii) JSP life cycle
(iii) Annotations and its types
(iv) Aspect-oriented programming

Master Of Computer Applications (MCA)
Chapter 5: Term-End Examination, December, 2023
MCS-220: Web Technologies

Time: 3 Hours
Maximum Marks: 100

Note:
(i) Question no. 1 is compulsory.
(ii) Attempt any three questions from the rest.

1. (a) What is J2EE? Briefly discuss the components of J2EE. (5 Marks)

(b) What is a servlet? Briefly discuss the lifecycle of a servlet. (5 Marks)

(c) Differentiate between session and cookie. Give a suitable example for each. (5 Marks)

(d) Write a JSP program for generating the Fibonacci series. Support your code with suitable comments. (5 Marks)

(e) What are Interceptors in Struts2? Briefly discuss the role of Interceptors in Struts2. (5 Marks)

(f) Differentiate between Spring Boot and Spring MVC. (5 Marks)

(g) Briefly discuss the term "Inversion of Control (IoC)". Also, draw a block diagram for IoC flow. (5 Marks)

(h) What is Custom CSS? How can Custom CSS be included in JSP? Discuss. (5 Marks)

2. (a) What is the need for application properties in Spring Boot? Explain how application properties of Spring Boot can be set through properties files, command-line arguments, and environment variables. (10 Marks)

(b) What is Hibernate? Briefly discuss the various states of the Hibernate Entity Life Cycle. Also, draw a block diagram for the same. (10 Marks)

3. (a) What is the relationship between JPA, Spring Data JPA, and Hibernate? Explain Eager and Lazy loading in Hibernate. How do Eager and Lazy loading improve the performance of Hibernate applications? (10 Marks)

(b) What is a Message Digest? How does a message digest differ from a message authentication code? Give characteristics of both. (10 Marks)

4. (a) Briefly discuss the following security vulnerabilities of any web app:

(i) Cross-Site Scripting (XSS)

(ii) Cross-Site Request Forgery (CSRF)

(iii) SQL Injection (SQLi)

(iv) Denial-of-Service (DoS)

(v) Insecure Direct Object References (IDOR) (10 Marks)

(b) Describe role-based login. Write a sample code to configure role-based login. (5 Marks)

(c) What is role-based access control? Write the simple configuration code to restrict URL access based on roles. (5 Marks)

5. Write short notes on the following: (5×4=20 Marks)

(i) Design Patterns
(ii) Servlet Collaboration
(iii) Components of JSP
(iv) Spring Framework

Chapter 6: Most Asked Questions Part-A

1. Explain the architecture of the World Wide Web and its key components.
Answer: The World Wide Web (WWW) operates on a client-server architecture where clients (web browsers) request resources from servers using HTTP/HTTPS protocols. Key components include web servers that host websites, web browsers that display content, and protocols like TCP/IP for communication. URLs identify resources, while DNS translates domain names to IP addresses. MCA graduates should understand how these components interact to deliver web content efficiently and securely to users worldwide.

2. Discuss the differences between static and dynamic web pages with examples.
Answer: Static web pages display fixed content and do not change unless manually updated, using technologies like HTML and CSS. Dynamic web pages, built with languages like PHP, ASP.NET, or JavaScript, generate content based on user interactions or database queries. For example, a portfolio website is static, while an e-commerce site showing personalized recommendations is dynamic. MCA graduates must learn both types to develop effective web solutions.

3. Explain the importance of HTML5 in modern web development.
Answer: HTML5 introduced semantic elements (e.g., `<header>`, `<article>`), multimedia support with `<audio>` and `<video>`, and offline capabilities via local storage and service workers. It enhances accessibility, SEO, and user experience without requiring external plugins like Flash. MCA graduates should master HTML5 to build responsive and interactive web applications compatible with modern browsers.

4. Discuss how CSS3 has transformed web design and layout management.
Answer: CSS3 introduced advanced features like animations, transitions, gradients, and flexbox/grid layouts. These capabilities allow developers to create responsive, visually appealing designs that adapt to various screen sizes. MCA graduates should utilize CSS3 to ensure consistent design aesthetics and enhance user engagement across devices.

5. Explain the working of JavaScript and its role in client-side scripting.
Answer: JavaScript is a scripting language that runs on the browser to add interactivity to web pages. It manipulates the Document Object Model (DOM) to update content dynamically, handle events, and validate forms. MCA graduates should understand JavaScript's importance in creating responsive user interfaces and enhancing user experience.

6. Discuss the advantages of using AJAX in web applications.
Answer: AJAX (Asynchronous JavaScript and XML) enables web applications to fetch data from servers without reloading the entire page. It improves user experience by enabling dynamic updates and faster interactions. MCA graduates should learn AJAX to develop modern web apps like Gmail, which rely on asynchronous communication for seamless functionality.

7. Explain the client-server model and how it applies to web technologies.
Answer: In the client-server model, clients send requests for resources, and servers respond with the requested data. Web browsers act as clients, and web servers like Apache or Nginx process these requests. MCA graduates must understand this model to design efficient web applications that handle multiple client requests simultaneously.

8. Discuss the differences between GET and POST methods in HTTP requests.
Answer: GET sends data via URL parameters and is used for retrieving resources, while POST sends data in the request body and is preferred for submitting sensitive or large data. MCA graduates should choose the appropriate method for tasks like form submissions, ensuring security and efficiency in data transfer.

9. Explain the purpose of web frameworks like Django and Angular in web development.
Answer: Web frameworks simplify development by providing reusable components and enforcing best practices. Django (Python) supports server-side development with built-in ORM and security features, while Angular

(JavaScript) enables building dynamic single-page applications (SPAs). MCA graduates should explore these frameworks to develop scalable and maintainable web apps.

10. Discuss the concept of RESTful web services and their significance.
Answer: REST (Representational State Transfer) uses standard HTTP methods (GET, POST, PUT, DELETE) to perform CRUD operations on resources. RESTful APIs are lightweight, scalable, and language-independent, making them ideal for modern web applications. MCA graduates should learn REST principles to integrate front-end and back-end systems effectively.

11. Explain the role of cookies, sessions, and local storage in web applications.
Answer: Cookies store small pieces of data on the client-side for tracking user preferences, while sessions store data on the server-side linked to a user session. Local storage provides larger client-side storage for modern web apps. MCA graduates should understand these mechanisms to manage state and enhance user experience securely.

12. Discuss the challenges of cross-browser compatibility and how to overcome them.
Answer: Cross-browser compatibility ensures web apps work consistently across different browsers. Challenges include varying support for HTML/CSS features and JavaScript APIs. MCA graduates should use CSS resets, vendor prefixes, and tools like Babel and polyfills to address these issues effectively.

13. Explain the importance of responsive web design in today's digital landscape.
Answer: Responsive web design ensures websites adapt to various screen sizes and devices using flexible grids and media queries. MCA graduates should prioritize responsiveness to deliver seamless user experiences across desktops, tablets, and smartphones, which is critical in a mobile-first world.

14. Discuss how HTTPS enhances web security compared to HTTP.
Answer: HTTPS encrypts data exchanged between clients and servers using SSL/TLS, protecting against eavesdropping and man-in-the-middle attacks. MCA graduates should enforce HTTPS to secure sensitive transactions like login and payment processes, ensuring user trust.

15. Explain the significance of search engine optimization (SEO) in web development.
Answer: SEO improves a website's visibility in search engine results, driving organic traffic. MCA graduates should implement best practices like semantic HTML, meta tags, and fast-loading pages to enhance discoverability and user engagement.

16. Describe the role of XML and JSON in data exchange for web applications.
Answer: XML (Extensible Markup Language) and JSON (JavaScript Object Notation) are widely used for data exchange between clients and servers. XML is verbose but supports complex data structures and is commonly used in legacy systems. JSON, being lightweight and easily parsed by JavaScript, is preferred in modern web applications for APIs. MCA graduates should master both formats as they are essential in RESTful APIs and cross-platform communication for web technologies.

17. Discuss the concept of progressive web apps (PWAs) and their advantages.
Answer: PWAs combine web and mobile app features, offering offline support, push notifications, and app-like interfaces. They are built using HTML, CSS, and JavaScript with service workers enabling caching and offline access. MCA graduates should explore PWAs to create lightweight, installable web apps that enhance user engagement without requiring app store distribution.

18. Explain the difference between client-side rendering and server-side rendering in web development.
Answer: Client-side rendering (CSR) loads a blank page and uses JavaScript to render content dynamically in the browser, while server-side rendering (SSR) generates and sends fully rendered HTML from the server. CSR offers better interactivity but slower initial load, while SSR improves SEO and faster initial rendering. MCA graduates should know when to use each approach for building high-performance web apps.

19. Discuss the significance of Content Delivery Networks (CDNs) in web performance.
Answer: CDNs distribute website content across multiple servers worldwide, enabling users to load resources from the nearest server location. This reduces latency, improves load times, and enhances scalability during traffic spikes.

MCA graduates should implement CDNs to optimize performance and provide a seamless experience to global users.

20. Explain the importance of form validation and methods to implement it.
Answer: Form validation ensures data entered by users is accurate and secure, preventing errors and malicious input. MCA graduates should use client-side validation (JavaScript) for quick feedback and server-side validation for security, employing techniques like regular expressions and built-in HTML5 validation attributes.

21. Discuss how responsive images improve website performance and user experience.
Answer: Responsive images adapt to different screen resolutions, ensuring optimal loading and display quality. MCA graduates should use HTML attributes like `srcset` and `sizes`, and formats like WebP to deliver lightweight images, improving page speed and user satisfaction on all devices.

22. Explain the role of the Document Object Model (DOM) in web programming.
Answer: The DOM represents a web page's structure as a tree of objects, allowing developers to manipulate content and styles dynamically with JavaScript. MCA graduates should understand DOM manipulation for tasks like updating elements, handling events, and creating interactive web pages.

23. Discuss the differences between synchronous and asynchronous JavaScript execution.
Answer: Synchronous JavaScript executes tasks sequentially, blocking the browser until each task completes, while asynchronous JavaScript allows other operations to continue using callbacks, promises, or async/await syntax. MCA graduates should master asynchronous programming to enhance web app responsiveness and avoid freezing the UI.

24. Explain how web sockets enable real-time communication in web applications.
Answer: WebSockets establish a persistent, bidirectional connection between client and server, enabling real-time updates. Unlike HTTP, which is request-response-based, WebSockets allow continuous data flow. MCA graduates should learn to implement WebSockets for use cases like chat apps, live notifications, and gaming platforms.

25. Discuss the importance of accessibility (a11y) in web development.
Answer: Accessibility ensures websites are usable by individuals with disabilities, promoting inclusivity. MCA graduates should follow standards like WCAG, use semantic HTML, ARIA attributes, and test with screen readers to create accessible web applications.

26. Explain the differences between relational databases and NoSQL databases in web technologies.
Answer: Relational databases (e.g., MySQL) use structured schemas and SQL for queries, while NoSQL databases (e.g., MongoDB) are schema-less and handle unstructured data efficiently. MCA graduates should understand their use cases to choose the right database for web apps with diverse data requirements.

27. Discuss how HTTPS certificates (SSL/TLS) work and their role in secure web communication.
Answer: SSL/TLS encrypts data between client and server to prevent eavesdropping and tampering. HTTPS certificates verify server authenticity, enabling secure communication. MCA graduates should implement HTTPS for all web applications to ensure user trust and meet modern security standards.

28. Explain the difference between Single Page Applications (SPAs) and Multi Page Applications (MPAs).
Answer: SPAs load a single HTML page and dynamically update content without reloading, while MPAs reload entire pages for navigation. SPAs, built with frameworks like React, provide seamless UX, whereas MPAs are easier for SEO. MCA graduates should weigh trade-offs when designing web architectures.

29. Discuss the purpose of REST API authentication methods such as API keys, OAuth, and JWT.
Answer: API keys are simple tokens for basic authentication, OAuth allows secure delegated access, and JWT (JSON Web Tokens) provide compact, secure user authentication. MCA graduates should understand these methods to protect APIs from unauthorized access.

30. Explain the benefits and challenges of using microservices in web applications.
Answer: Microservices break applications into small, independent services, improving scalability and maintainability. However, they introduce challenges like complex deployment and inter-service communication.

MCA graduates should explore tools like Docker and Kubernetes for managing microservices architectures effectively.

31. Discuss how search engines index web pages and the role of sitemaps in SEO.
Answer: Search engines crawl web pages using bots, indexing content for search results. Sitemaps guide crawlers to important pages and improve SEO by ensuring proper discovery. MCA graduates should create XML sitemaps to enhance website visibility.

32. Explain the purpose of responsive typography in modern web design.
Answer: Responsive typography adjusts text size, line height, and spacing to enhance readability across devices. MCA graduates should use relative units (em, rem, vw) and media queries to create visually appealing and accessible designs.

33. Discuss the concept of cross-site scripting (XSS) and prevention techniques.
Answer: XSS attacks inject malicious scripts into web pages, compromising user data. MCA graduates should sanitize user inputs, use Content Security Policy (CSP), and employ frameworks that auto-escape outputs to prevent XSS vulnerabilities.

34. Explain how to implement lazy loading for images and resources in web applications.
Answer: Lazy loading delays loading of off-screen images until users scroll to them, reducing initial load time. MCA graduates should use the `loading="lazy"` attribute in HTML and libraries for complex scenarios to optimize performance.

35. Discuss the role of APIs in integrating third-party services into web applications.
Answer: APIs allow web apps to access external services like payment gateways, social logins, and maps. MCA graduates should learn to consume REST and GraphQL APIs securely for building feature-rich applications.

36. Explain the importance of web performance optimization and tools used for it.
Answer: Optimizing performance reduces load times and improves user experience. MCA graduates should use tools like Lighthouse and WebPageTest to audit and improve metrics like page speed, minimizing HTTP requests, and enabling compression.

37. Discuss the concept of web caching and its impact on performance.
Answer: Web caching stores copies of resources to serve them quickly on subsequent requests. MCA graduates should use browser caching, server-side caching, and CDNs to enhance performance and reduce server load.

38. Explain the difference between HTML, XHTML, and XML in web technologies.
Answer: HTML is lenient with syntax and focuses on display, XHTML is stricter with XML-like syntax, and XML is used for data storage and transport. MCA graduates should know where each is applied in modern web solutions.

39. Discuss the role of web analytics in improving website effectiveness.
Answer: Web analytics track user interactions and behavior on websites. MCA graduates should use tools like Google Analytics to analyze traffic, identify issues, and optimize content for higher engagement and conversions.

40. Explain the use of web workers in improving browser performance.
Answer: Web workers run JavaScript in the background without blocking the main thread, enabling smoother user interfaces. MCA graduates should use web workers for heavy computations to keep web apps responsive.

41. Discuss the difference between relative and absolute URLs in web development.
Answer: Relative URLs are based on the location of the current page, while absolute URLs include the full path. MCA graduates should use relative URLs for internal linking and absolute URLs when referencing external resources or for SEO consistency.

42. Explain the use of media queries in responsive web design.
Answer: Media queries apply CSS rules based on device characteristics like width, height, or orientation. MCA graduates should use them to ensure web designs adapt to different screen sizes, improving usability across devices.

43. Discuss the significance of favicon and meta tags in web development.
Answer: Favicons improve brand recognition in browser tabs, while meta tags provide metadata for search engines and social sharing. MCA graduates should implement these to enhance SEO and user experience.

44. Explain the concept of service workers in PWAs and their benefits.
Answer: Service workers enable offline functionality, caching, and background sync in PWAs. MCA graduates should learn service workers to build web apps that work reliably even without a constant internet connection.

45. Discuss the importance of web standards and validation in modern development.
Answer: Web standards ensure cross-browser compatibility and accessibility. MCA graduates should validate HTML/CSS using W3C tools to adhere to standards, improving maintainability and user experience.

46. Explain the differences between inline, internal, and external CSS.
Answer: Inline CSS applies styles directly to elements, internal CSS defines styles in `<style>` tags, and external CSS links to separate stylesheet files. MCA graduates should prefer external CSS for scalability and cleaner code.

47. Discuss the purpose of minification and bundling in web development.
Answer: Minification removes unnecessary characters from code, and bundling combines multiple files, reducing HTTP requests. MCA graduates should use tools like Webpack to optimize web app delivery.

48. Explain how to use ARIA roles to improve accessibility in web applications.
Answer: ARIA (Accessible Rich Internet Applications) roles define element purposes for assistive technologies. MCA graduates should use ARIA attributes to enhance screen reader support, ensuring inclusive web designs.

49. Discuss the differences between HTTP/1.1 and HTTP/2 protocols.
Answer: HTTP/2 supports multiplexing, header compression, and server push, offering faster and more efficient data transfer than HTTP/1.1. MCA graduates should adopt HTTP/2 for improved web performance.

50. Explain the concept of web application security testing and its key components.
Answer: Web application security testing identifies vulnerabilities like XSS, CSRF, and SQL injection. MCA graduates should use tools like OWASP ZAP and Burp Suite to perform thorough security assessments, ensuring applications are robust against attacks.

51. Discuss the purpose of web application firewalls (WAF) in securing web applications.
Answer: A Web Application Firewall (WAF) filters and monitors HTTP traffic to and from a web application, protecting it from common attacks like SQL injection, cross-site scripting (XSS), and DDoS. MCA graduates should understand how WAFs act as a shield between users and servers, analyzing traffic patterns to block malicious requests and ensuring compliance with security policies. WAFs are critical for maintaining data integrity and ensuring application availability in high-traffic web environments.

52. Explain the role of server-side scripting languages in dynamic web development.
Answer: Server-side scripting languages like PHP, Python, and Node.js generate dynamic content based on user inputs or database queries. Unlike client-side scripts, which execute in browsers, these scripts run on the server and send pre-processed HTML to the client. MCA graduates should learn these languages to develop interactive and data-driven web applications that handle tasks like user authentication, form processing, and content management securely.

53. Discuss the significance of Content Security Policy (CSP) in preventing web attacks.
Answer: CSP is a security standard that helps prevent cross-site scripting (XSS) and data injection attacks by controlling the resources a web page can load. MCA graduates should learn to configure CSP headers to restrict inline scripts, external resource loading, and unauthorized domains, significantly enhancing web application security.

54. Explain the concept of cross-origin resource sharing (CORS) and its importance.
Answer: CORS is a security feature implemented in browsers that controls how web applications request resources from different origins. MCA graduates should understand how configuring CORS headers properly allows

legitimate cross-origin requests while preventing unauthorized data access, ensuring secure API integration in modern web applications.

55. Discuss how web developers can improve website loading speed using optimization techniques.
Answer: Website speed is critical for user experience and SEO. MCA graduates should use techniques like image compression, minification of CSS/JS, lazy loading, and caching strategies. Implementing CDN services and reducing HTTP requests also significantly improves page load times and user retention.

56. Explain the importance of browser developer tools in debugging web applications.
Answer: Browser developer tools, such as Chrome DevTools, allow developers to inspect and debug HTML, CSS, and JavaScript in real-time. MCA graduates should use features like network monitoring, console logging, and performance profiling to identify and fix issues efficiently during development.

57. Discuss the concept of web APIs and how they enhance functionality in web applications.
Answer: Web APIs enable applications to communicate with external services, allowing integration of features like maps, payment gateways, and social media logins. MCA graduates should understand REST and GraphQL APIs to build scalable, modular, and interactive web applications.

58. Explain how web developers can ensure compatibility across multiple devices and browsers.
Answer: Ensuring compatibility requires testing applications on various devices and browsers to address rendering differences. MCA graduates should use responsive design principles, CSS vendor prefixes, and cross-browser testing tools like BrowserStack to deliver consistent user experiences.

59. Discuss the role of JSON Web Tokens (JWT) in secure authentication systems.
Answer: JWT is a compact, URL-safe token format used to securely transmit information between parties. MCA graduates should learn how JWT facilitates stateless authentication in modern web applications, reducing server load while maintaining secure user sessions.

60. Explain the differences between session storage and local storage in web browsers.
Answer: Session storage retains data only for the duration of a page session, while local storage persists data even after the browser closes. MCA graduates should understand their use cases in storing user preferences, form data, or caching lightweight application data securely.

61. Discuss the advantages of using web components in modern front-end development.
Answer: Web components enable developers to create reusable, encapsulated custom elements. MCA graduates should explore standards like Shadow DOM, HTML templates, and custom elements to build modular, maintainable front-end architectures that work across frameworks.

62. Explain how to secure forms in web applications against CSRF attacks.
Answer: CSRF (Cross-Site Request Forgery) tricks users into performing unintended actions. MCA graduates should implement anti-CSRF tokens, use SameSite cookies, and verify user intent to protect forms from such attacks effectively.

63. Discuss the significance of semantic HTML in accessibility and SEO.
Answer: Semantic HTML tags like `<header>`, `<article>`, and `<footer>` convey meaning to assistive technologies and search engines. MCA graduates should use these tags to improve website accessibility for users with disabilities and enhance SEO rankings.

64. Explain how asynchronous JavaScript functions improve web application performance.
Answer: Asynchronous JavaScript functions prevent blocking of the main thread, allowing simultaneous operations like API calls and UI rendering. MCA graduates should use Promises, async/await syntax, and fetch APIs for building smooth, responsive web experiences.

65. Discuss the role of web sockets in enabling real-time web applications.

Answer: WebSockets establish a persistent connection between client and server, enabling bidirectional communication. MCA graduates should implement WebSockets for chat applications, live notifications, and collaborative tools requiring real-time updates.

66. Explain how to implement OAuth 2.0 for secure third-party authentication.
Answer: OAuth 2.0 is an authorization framework that allows users to grant limited access to their data without sharing credentials. MCA graduates should learn OAuth workflows, including authorization code flow, to integrate social logins and APIs securely in web applications.

67. Discuss the challenges of developing multilingual web applications.
Answer: Multilingual applications require handling translations, cultural nuances, and encoding issues. MCA graduates should use libraries like i18next and ensure proper design for text expansion to build inclusive global applications.

68. Explain how CDN edge caching improves web application scalability.
Answer: CDN edge caching stores resources on servers closer to users, reducing latency and server load. MCA graduates should leverage CDNs to scale applications and provide faster access to static assets during high traffic.

69. Discuss how to prevent clickjacking attacks in web applications.
Answer: Clickjacking tricks users into clicking hidden elements. MCA graduates should use X-Frame-Options and Content Security Policy (CSP) headers to prevent their sites from being embedded in iframes on malicious domains.

70. Explain the concept of headless CMS and its benefits in web development.
Answer: A headless CMS decouples content management from front-end delivery, enabling content to be served via APIs. MCA graduates should explore headless CMS platforms to build flexible, multi-channel web applications.

71. Discuss how browser caching works and its role in improving web performance.
Answer: Browser caching stores resources locally, reducing the need to fetch them repeatedly from servers. MCA graduates should configure cache-control headers effectively to enhance load times and reduce bandwidth usage.

72. Explain the role of service workers in enabling offline capabilities in web apps.
Answer: Service workers act as proxies between web apps and networks, allowing caching and offline support. MCA graduates should implement service workers for Progressive Web Apps (PWAs) to enhance resilience and user experience.

73. Discuss the advantages of using GraphQL over REST APIs in modern web apps.
Answer: GraphQL allows clients to request only needed data, reducing over-fetching and improving performance. MCA graduates should explore GraphQL for building flexible APIs and optimizing data transfer in complex applications.

74. Explain how to handle file uploads securely in web applications.
Answer: Secure file uploads prevent malware and server overloads. MCA graduates should validate file types, enforce size limits, scan for viruses, and store uploads in restricted directories to mitigate security risks.

75. Discuss the concept of DOM event delegation and its advantages.
Answer: Event delegation attaches a single event listener to a parent element, handling events for its child elements. MCA graduates should use this technique to improve performance and manage dynamically added elements efficiently.

76. Explain the role of WebAssembly in enhancing web application performance.
Answer: WebAssembly allows high-performance code (e.g., C/C++) to run in browsers alongside JavaScript. MCA graduates should explore WebAssembly for computationally intensive web apps like games and image editors.

77. Discuss how to secure REST APIs against common vulnerabilities.
Answer: Securing REST APIs involves authentication, rate limiting, input validation, and HTTPS. MCA graduates should use tools like API gateways and implement OAuth/JWT to protect APIs from unauthorized access.

78. Explain the differences between cookies, local storage, and indexedDB.
Answer: Cookies store small amounts of data for server communication, local storage offers larger storage for simple key-value pairs, while IndexedDB supports complex data structures. MCA graduates should choose the right mechanism based on storage needs and security considerations.

79. Discuss the purpose of prefetching and preloading in web performance optimization.
Answer: Prefetching and preloading hint the browser to load resources in advance. MCA graduates should use `<link rel="prefetch">` and `<link rel="preload">` to improve user experience by reducing perceived load times.

80. Explain the use of webhooks in modern web applications.
Answer: Webhooks allow apps to receive real-time notifications when events occur on external systems. MCA graduates should implement webhooks for features like payment status updates or chat integrations in web applications.

81. Discuss how accessibility testing tools help in building inclusive web apps.
Answer: Tools like Axe, Lighthouse, and WAVE evaluate web accessibility for users with disabilities. MCA graduates should integrate these tools into workflows to identify and fix accessibility issues proactively.

82. Explain the purpose of minification and tree-shaking in front-end optimization.
Answer: Minification removes unnecessary characters, and tree-shaking eliminates unused code. MCA graduates should use tools like Webpack to reduce file sizes, ensuring faster front-end performance.

83. Discuss the importance of web security headers in protecting web applications.
Answer: Security headers like HSTS, X-Content-Type-Options, and X-Frame-Options prevent attacks such as XSS and clickjacking. MCA graduates should configure these headers correctly for enhanced web application security.

84. Explain how content delivery strategies impact SEO performance.
Answer: Delivery strategies like lazy loading, CDN usage, and server-side rendering influence SEO. MCA graduates should balance performance optimizations with SEO best practices to maintain crawlability and ranking.

85. Discuss how to use ARIA landmarks to improve web accessibility.
Answer: ARIA landmarks define page regions for assistive technologies. MCA graduates should use roles like `banner`, `main`, and `navigation` to enhance accessibility and navigation for screen reader users.

86. Explain how to configure secure headers to prevent MIME type sniffing attacks.
Answer: MCA graduates should use the `X-Content-Type-Options: nosniff` header to enforce declared content types, preventing browsers from guessing MIME types and executing malicious files.

87. Discuss the role of critical rendering path optimization in web development.
Answer: Optimizing the critical rendering path reduces the time from page load to first paint. MCA graduates should minimize CSS and defer non-essential scripts to enhance perceived web performance.

88. Explain how to prevent data leakage in Single Page Applications (SPAs).
Answer: SPAs may inadvertently expose sensitive data in client-side code. MCA graduates should use secure APIs, avoid storing secrets in front-end code, and enforce proper authentication mechanisms to mitigate data leakage risks.

89. Discuss how browser preconnect and DNS-prefetch improve web loading speed.
Answer: Preconnect and DNS-prefetch reduce connection setup time for external resources. MCA graduates should use `<link rel="preconnect">` for critical domains to enhance performance.

90. Explain how to handle CORS preflight requests in APIs.
Answer: Preflight requests check server permissions for cross-origin requests. MCA graduates should configure servers with appropriate CORS headers, specifying allowed methods, origins, and credentials to enable secure API access.

91. Discuss the significance of lazy rendering in improving web application performance.
Answer: Lazy rendering defers loading non-critical components until needed. MCA graduates should implement this technique to improve initial load times, particularly in SPAs with large UI components.

92. Explain the concept of critical CSS and how it improves page load speed.
Answer: Critical CSS includes only above-the-fold styles in the initial load. MCA graduates should extract and inline critical CSS for faster rendering, improving performance metrics like First Contentful Paint (FCP).

93. Discuss the role of browser push notifications in modern web apps.
Answer: Push notifications engage users by delivering timely updates even when the browser is closed. MCA graduates should implement push APIs responsibly, ensuring users can opt in and out to avoid spamming.

94. Explain how to handle race conditions in asynchronous JavaScript code.
Answer: Race conditions occur when the timing of asynchronous operations leads to unexpected outcomes. MCA graduates should use Promises, async/await, and proper sequencing to prevent conflicts and ensure reliable code execution.

95. Discuss the benefits of using HTTPS/2 multiplexing for modern websites.
Answer: Multiplexing in HTTP/2 allows multiple requests to share a single connection, reducing latency and improving performance. MCA graduates should migrate to HTTP/2 to enhance modern website delivery efficiency.

96. Explain the differences between progressive rendering and full-page rendering.
Answer: Progressive rendering displays parts of a web page as they load, improving perceived performance, while full-page rendering waits until all content is ready. MCA graduates should implement progressive rendering for better user experiences.

97. Discuss how to use the viewport meta tag in responsive web design.
Answer: The viewport meta tag controls how a page scales on mobile devices. MCA graduates should configure it properly to ensure layouts adapt fluidly across screen sizes.

98. Explain how to handle stale cache issues in web applications.
Answer: Stale cache can serve outdated content to users. MCA graduates should implement cache busting techniques like versioned URLs or service worker updates to ensure users receive the latest resources.

99. Discuss the role of webhooks in real-time data synchronization across systems.
Answer: Webhooks notify external systems instantly when events occur. MCA graduates should use them for real-time synchronization in applications like payment gateways or CRM tools.

100. Explain how to design REST APIs for high availability and scalability.
Answer: Designing scalable REST APIs involves stateless architecture, load balancing, and caching strategies. MCA graduates should implement rate limiting and distributed systems to ensure APIs remain highly available under heavy traffic.

101. Discuss the importance of HTTP status codes in web development.
Answer: HTTP status codes are responses sent by servers to indicate the outcome of client requests. Codes like 200 (OK), 404 (Not Found), and 500 (Server Error) help developers debug and handle errors effectively. MCA graduates should understand how to use these codes in API responses and web applications to provide clear communication between the server and client while improving user experience and search engine indexing.

102. Explain the role of asynchronous event loops in JavaScript.
Answer: The JavaScript event loop handles asynchronous operations, allowing non-blocking code execution. It places tasks like API calls or timers into queues and processes them after the main stack is clear. MCA graduates should understand the event loop to write efficient asynchronous code that keeps web applications responsive.

103. Discuss the differences between relative, fixed, and sticky positioning in CSS.

Answer: Relative positioning shifts elements based on their normal position, fixed positioning anchors elements relative to the viewport, and sticky positioning toggles between relative and fixed based on scroll. MCA graduates should learn these techniques to design layouts with dynamic behaviors and enhanced usability.

104. Explain how the Fetch API simplifies data fetching in web applications.
Answer: The Fetch API provides a modern, promise-based approach to making HTTP requests, replacing older methods like XMLHttpRequest. MCA graduates should use Fetch for cleaner, more readable code when working with APIs or handling server communication in web applications.

105. Discuss the role of JSON-LD in enhancing SEO for web pages.
Answer: JSON-LD (JavaScript Object Notation for Linked Data) helps structure data for search engines to understand website content better. MCA graduates should use JSON-LD to add rich snippets like ratings, events, or product details, improving visibility in search results.

106. Explain the importance of critical CSS and above-the-fold rendering.
Answer: Critical CSS contains styles needed to render visible content immediately. MCA graduates should extract and inline critical CSS for faster page load times, improving metrics like First Contentful Paint (FCP) and overall user experience.

107. Discuss how responsive navigation menus improve mobile usability.
Answer: Responsive menus adapt to small screens using techniques like hamburger icons or collapsible lists. MCA graduates should design such menus to enhance usability on mobile devices, ensuring intuitive navigation without overwhelming users.

108. Explain how HTTP/3 and QUIC improve web performance over HTTP/2.
Answer: HTTP/3, built on the QUIC protocol, reduces latency and connection setup times by using UDP instead of TCP. MCA graduates should explore HTTP/3 for faster, more reliable web application performance, especially in high-latency networks.

109. Discuss the importance of using a version control system (VCS) like Git in web development projects.
Answer: VCS tools like Git track changes in code, enabling collaboration, rollback, and branching workflows. MCA graduates should master Git to manage source code efficiently, prevent conflicts, and ensure smooth teamwork in web development.

110. Explain the concept of deferred and async attributes in loading JavaScript files.
Answer: The `defer` attribute delays script execution until HTML parsing is complete, while `async` executes scripts as soon as they are downloaded. MCA graduates should use these attributes to prevent blocking rendering and improve web page performance.

111. Discuss the role of HTTPS Strict Transport Security (HSTS) in web security.
Answer: HSTS enforces secure HTTPS connections, preventing downgrade attacks. MCA graduates should configure HSTS headers to ensure web applications always use encrypted channels, enhancing security against man-in-the-middle attacks.

112. Explain how to create animations in web applications using CSS transitions and keyframes.
Answer: CSS transitions animate changes between states, while keyframes define complex animations. MCA graduates should use these tools to create engaging, smooth animations that enhance user interfaces without relying on JavaScript.

113. Discuss how responsive tables are implemented in web design.
Answer: Responsive tables adapt to small screens using techniques like horizontal scrolling, stacking, or hiding non-essential columns. MCA graduates should use CSS media queries and frameworks like Bootstrap to design tables that remain usable on all devices.

114. Explain the difference between absolute and relative paths in linking resources.

Answer: Absolute paths include the full URL or root directory path, while relative paths are based on the current file's location. MCA graduates should choose appropriately to manage resource linking efficiently in web projects.

115. Discuss the role of the Shadow DOM in encapsulating web component styles.
Answer: The Shadow DOM isolates styles and markup for web components, preventing conflicts with global styles. MCA graduates should use this feature for building reusable, self-contained components in modern front-end frameworks.

116. Explain the concept of throttling and debouncing in event handling.
Answer: Throttling limits function calls to a fixed interval, while debouncing delays execution until a specified pause in events. MCA graduates should apply these techniques to optimize performance when handling frequent events like scrolling or resizing.

117. Discuss how to use CSS variables for maintaining consistent design systems.
Answer: CSS variables (custom properties) store reusable values like colors or spacing, enabling easier theme management. MCA graduates should use them to create scalable and maintainable stylesheets for web projects.

118. Explain how browser caching strategies impact dynamic web content delivery.
Answer: Caching strategies like Cache-Control headers and service workers help serve static assets quickly while managing dynamic content freshness. MCA graduates should design appropriate strategies to balance performance and data accuracy.

119. Discuss the use of web storage APIs in modern web applications.
Answer: Web storage APIs like localStorage and sessionStorage provide lightweight key-value data storage in browsers. MCA graduates should use them for persisting user preferences, caching data, and supporting offline functionalities.

120. Explain the purpose of media types and breakpoints in CSS.
Answer: Media types target devices (screen, print), and breakpoints define layout changes at specific widths. MCA graduates should combine these to create responsive designs that adapt fluidly across devices.

121. Discuss how SVG graphics improve scalability and resolution in web design.
Answer: SVGs are vector-based, scaling without loss of quality on any screen resolution. MCA graduates should use SVGs for logos, icons, and animations to ensure crisp visuals across devices.

122. Explain the role of ARIA attributes in enhancing accessibility.
Answer: ARIA (Accessible Rich Internet Applications) attributes describe roles, states, and properties to assistive technologies. MCA graduates should apply ARIA attributes to improve web accessibility for users relying on screen readers.

123. Discuss the differences between session-based and token-based authentication.
Answer: Session-based authentication stores credentials on the server, while token-based (e.g., JWT) stores them on the client. MCA graduates should understand their trade-offs in scalability, security, and use cases for modern web apps.

124. Explain how web developers can prevent DOM-based XSS vulnerabilities.
Answer: DOM-based XSS occurs when client-side scripts process untrusted input. MCA graduates should sanitize inputs, avoid `innerHTML`, and use safe APIs like `textContent` to mitigate risks.

125. Discuss the role of web accessibility audits in improving user experience.
Answer: Accessibility audits evaluate how well a website supports users with disabilities. MCA graduates should conduct audits using tools like Axe and manual testing to identify barriers and implement improvements, ensuring inclusivity.

Chapter 7: Most Asked Questions Part-B

1. Analyze how a web developer can improve the performance of an e-commerce website during high traffic sales events.

Answer: During high traffic, e-commerce websites face slowdowns and potential crashes. Developers should implement load balancing to distribute requests evenly across servers. Using a Content Delivery Network (CDN) reduces latency by serving assets from edge servers. Techniques like lazy loading images, compressing files, and caching static resources also improve performance. MCA graduates must optimize database queries and use asynchronous processing for tasks like sending emails to ensure smooth functioning during peak demand.

2. Discuss how to design a secure login system for a web application to prevent brute-force attacks.

Answer: A secure login system uses measures like account lockouts after multiple failed attempts and CAPTCHA challenges to block bots. MCA graduates should enforce strong password policies, hash passwords using algorithms like bcrypt, and use HTTPS to encrypt credentials in transit. Rate limiting and monitoring suspicious activities further enhance protection against brute-force attacks, ensuring users' accounts remain secure.

3. Explain how you would integrate a third-party payment gateway into a web application securely.

Answer: To securely integrate a payment gateway, MCA graduates should use APIs provided by trusted providers like PayPal or Stripe. Sensitive data, like card details, should never pass through the server; instead, tokenization or hosted payment pages should be used. Enabling HTTPS, validating API responses, and adhering to PCI DSS standards ensure compliance and secure transaction handling.

4. Analyze the role of Progressive Web Apps (PWAs) in delivering seamless offline experiences.

Answer: PWAs use service workers to cache essential resources, allowing users to interact with applications offline or in poor network conditions. MCA graduates should design apps with fallback mechanisms for offline data storage using IndexedDB. Features like background sync update data once the connection is restored, creating a near-native experience for users while increasing engagement.

5. Discuss how you would prevent Cross-Site Scripting (XSS) attacks in a blog web application.

Answer: To prevent XSS, MCA graduates should sanitize user inputs by escaping HTML characters and using libraries like DOMPurify. Content Security Policy (CSP) headers should be implemented to block unauthorized scripts. Validating and encoding user-generated content ensures scripts cannot be injected, protecting readers from malicious payloads.

6. Explain how WebSockets can be used to build a real-time collaborative document editor.

Answer: WebSockets enable a persistent connection between clients and servers, facilitating instant updates in collaborative environments. MCA graduates should design systems where document changes are broadcasted to all connected users in real-time. Techniques like operational transformation or conflict-free replicated data types (CRDTs) ensure consistency and resolve editing conflicts.

7. Analyze the security risks of storing sensitive user data in local storage and how to mitigate them.

Answer: Local storage is vulnerable to XSS attacks as data is accessible through JavaScript. MCA graduates should avoid storing sensitive information like authentication tokens. Instead, use HTTP-only cookies or encrypt data before storage. Regularly sanitizing inputs and using CSPs further mitigate risks.

8. Discuss how responsive web design impacts accessibility for users with disabilities.

Answer: Responsive designs improve accessibility by ensuring layouts adapt across devices and screen readers work effectively. MCA graduates should use relative units, semantic HTML, and ARIA roles to enhance compatibility with assistive technologies, making web apps more inclusive for users with visual or motor impairments.

9. Explain how to implement two-factor authentication (2FA) in a web application.

Answer: 2FA adds a security layer by requiring users to provide a second credential, like an OTP sent via SMS or email. MCA graduates should integrate libraries for generating TOTP (Time-based One-Time Passwords) and ensure secure transmission using HTTPS. Backup codes and multi-device support enhance usability while maintaining strong security.

10. Analyze how to design an API rate-limiting strategy for a public REST API.
Answer: API rate limiting prevents abuse by restricting the number of requests per client over a period. MCA graduates should use token buckets or sliding window algorithms to implement limits. Providing informative error messages and allowing burst traffic within limits enhances user experience without compromising API stability.

11. Discuss how web developers can optimize single-page applications (SPAs) for SEO.
Answer: SPAs load content dynamically, which search engines may struggle to index. MCA graduates should use server-side rendering (SSR) or prerendering to generate static HTML pages for crawlers. Implementing proper meta tags and structured data further boosts SEO performance.

12. Explain how to build a scalable chat application using Node.js and Socket.IO.
Answer: Node.js supports high concurrency with its non-blocking I/O model, and Socket.IO simplifies WebSocket integration. MCA graduates should design the app with load balancers, use Redis for message queues, and ensure user authentication to handle large-scale real-time communication securely.

13. Analyze the ethical considerations of implementing location tracking in ride-sharing apps.
Answer: Location tracking enhances ride-matching efficiency but raises privacy concerns. MCA graduates should obtain user consent, anonymize location data, and provide opt-out options to respect user autonomy while maintaining functionality.

14. Discuss how web developers can improve perceived performance using skeleton screens.
Answer: Skeleton screens display placeholders while content loads, giving users a sense of progress. MCA graduates should use CSS animations for lightweight implementation, reducing perceived latency and improving user satisfaction on slower networks.

15. Explain how to secure REST APIs with JSON Web Tokens (JWT).
Answer: JWTs authenticate users without server-side session storage, improving scalability. MCA graduates should use signed tokens with short expiration times, refresh tokens for reauthentication, and HTTPS to prevent interception. Validating tokens on every request ensures secure API access.

16. Analyze how browser caching strategies can improve user experience in news websites.
Answer: Browser caching stores static assets locally, reducing repeated downloads. MCA graduates should use cache-control headers and service workers to cache frequently accessed content like logos and CSS. For dynamic content, techniques like stale-while-revalidate ensure freshness without sacrificing speed.

17. Discuss how to prevent SQL injection in a user registration form.
Answer: SQL injection exploits unsanitized inputs. MCA graduates should use parameterized queries or ORM frameworks to separate data from SQL logic. Validating user inputs and applying least privilege principles to database accounts further protect against injection attacks.

18. Explain how to design a multi-tenant SaaS web application.
Answer: Multi-tenant SaaS apps serve multiple clients on shared infrastructure. MCA graduates should implement data isolation strategies like row-level security or separate schemas and design APIs with tenant-aware authentication to ensure data privacy and scalability.

19. Analyze the role of accessibility audits in improving e-learning platforms.
Answer: Accessibility audits identify barriers for users with disabilities, such as missing alt text or improper heading structures. MCA graduates should use tools like Axe and manual testing to ensure e-learning platforms comply with WCAG standards, making education inclusive.

20. Discuss how to integrate social media authentication in a web application.
Answer: Social authentication allows users to log in with accounts from providers like Google or Facebook. MCA graduates should use OAuth 2.0 protocols to securely request and manage user permissions, minimizing barriers to entry while protecting user data.

21. Explain how to use GraphQL in building a content-rich web application.
Answer: GraphQL allows clients to request only the data they need, reducing over-fetching. MCA graduates should design flexible schemas and resolvers, leveraging GraphQL for faster, more efficient data fetching in content-heavy apps like blogs or dashboards.

22. Analyze how content delivery networks (CDNs) enhance security against DDoS attacks.
Answer: CDNs distribute traffic across global servers, absorbing and mitigating DDoS attacks. MCA graduates should enable CDN features like rate limiting and Web Application Firewalls (WAFs) to protect web apps from traffic spikes and malicious requests.

23. Discuss how to build an offline-first web application for rural areas with poor connectivity.
Answer: Offline-first apps cache data locally and sync with servers when online. MCA graduates should use IndexedDB and service workers to provide seamless user experiences in low-bandwidth regions, supporting rural digital inclusion efforts.

24. Explain how to implement CAPTCHA in a web application to prevent bot registrations.
Answer: CAPTCHAs distinguish human users from bots by presenting challenges like image selection or text recognition. MCA graduates should integrate reCAPTCHA APIs for effective bot prevention without disrupting user experience.

25. Analyze the ethical implications of personalized advertisements in web applications.
Answer: Personalized ads improve engagement but raise privacy concerns over user profiling. MCA graduates should obtain consent, provide ad preferences, and anonymize user data to balance personalization with ethical practices and compliance with regulations like GDPR.

26. Discuss how web developers can prevent data breaches in multi-user web applications.
Answer: Multi-user applications are vulnerable to unauthorized data access. MCA graduates should implement role-based access control (RBAC) to restrict permissions, encrypt sensitive data in transit and at rest, and sanitize all user inputs to avoid injection attacks. Regular vulnerability scans and secure session management techniques like short-lived tokens reduce the risk of breaches, ensuring user data remains protected in shared environments.

27. Explain how to design a content management system (CMS) for small businesses.
Answer: A CMS for small businesses should prioritize ease of use, allowing non-technical users to update content. MCA graduates should design an admin panel with rich text editors, media upload capabilities, and customizable templates. Security measures like user authentication and plugin sandboxing ensure safety, while a modular architecture supports scalability as business needs grow.

28. Analyze the challenges of integrating a live chat feature into an existing e-commerce platform.
Answer: Live chat enhances customer support but introduces technical and operational challenges. MCA graduates should design scalable real-time communication using WebSockets, ensure data privacy through secure message encryption, and provide seamless integration with CRM tools. Load testing ensures chat performance under heavy traffic, and fallback mechanisms like email escalation improve reliability.

29. Discuss how to optimize API calls for a mobile-first web application.
Answer: Optimizing API calls reduces latency and conserves bandwidth on mobile networks. MCA graduates should implement pagination, caching, and data compression (e.g., GZIP). Using GraphQL instead of REST avoids over-fetching, allowing mobile apps to request only necessary fields. Optimized APIs improve performance and user satisfaction in bandwidth-constrained environments.

30. Explain how to prevent cross-site request forgery (CSRF) in a web-based financial portal.
Answer: CSRF exploits authenticated user sessions to perform unauthorized actions. MCA graduates should implement anti-CSRF tokens, validate the origin header of incoming requests, and use SameSite cookie attributes. These measures protect sensitive financial operations like fund transfers from malicious requests.

31. Analyze how web developers can ensure compliance with GDPR in user-centric applications.

Answer: GDPR requires explicit user consent for data collection and processing. MCA graduates should implement consent banners, allow data portability and deletion, and maintain transparent privacy policies. Storing only necessary data and encrypting it ensures compliance while building user trust in web applications.

32. Discuss how to secure an API gateway for a microservices-based architecture.
Answer: API gateways centralize communication between clients and microservices, making them critical security points. MCA graduates should enforce authentication (OAuth2 or JWT), enable rate limiting, and monitor traffic for anomalies. Using HTTPS for encrypted communication and implementing API keys prevents unauthorized access to services.

33. Explain how you would implement dark mode in a modern web application.
Answer: Dark mode enhances user comfort, especially in low-light environments. MCA graduates should use CSS custom properties (variables) to define color themes and media queries like `prefers-color-scheme` to detect user preferences. Providing a toggle button with settings saved in local storage enhances user control over the interface.

34. Analyze the ethical challenges of using AI-based content filters in social media platforms.
Answer: AI filters reduce harmful content but may wrongly censor legitimate posts or exhibit bias. MCA graduates should design systems with transparent criteria, allow user appeals, and involve human moderators for edge cases. Ethical deployment requires balancing free expression with safety.

35. Discuss how to build a web-based video streaming platform optimized for low bandwidth areas.
Answer: To serve users in low-bandwidth regions, MCA graduates should implement adaptive bitrate streaming to adjust video quality dynamically. Caching frequently accessed content on edge servers using CDNs reduces latency. Offline download features and efficient video codecs like H.265 ensure accessibility even with limited connectivity.

36. Explain how to prevent man-in-the-middle (MITM) attacks in a web application.
Answer: MITM attacks intercept and alter communication between clients and servers. MCA graduates should enforce HTTPS using valid SSL/TLS certificates, implement HSTS headers, and use secure DNS protocols (DNS over HTTPS). Regularly updating libraries and frameworks also protects against known vulnerabilities.

37. Analyze the benefits and challenges of using a headless CMS for a news website.
Answer: Headless CMSs separate content from presentation, enabling multi-channel delivery (web, mobile, IoT). MCA graduates should leverage APIs for flexibility and scalability but address challenges like increased front-end complexity and potential security concerns with API exposure.

38. Discuss how you would implement rate limiting on a login API to prevent credential stuffing attacks.
Answer: Rate limiting restricts the number of login attempts per user or IP in a given time frame. MCA graduates should implement exponential backoff, CAPTCHA challenges after repeated failures, and IP blacklisting for malicious patterns. Logging and monitoring alert admins about suspicious activity.

39. Explain how web developers can optimize a Progressive Web App (PWA) for performance.
Answer: PWAs benefit from service workers caching assets for offline access. MCA graduates should implement precaching for critical resources, lazy loading for non-essential content, and background sync for seamless user experiences. Optimizing images and minimizing JavaScript bundles further improves performance.

40. Analyze the role of ethical design in gamification features for educational web platforms.
Answer: Gamification motivates learners but risks fostering unhealthy competition or addiction. MCA graduates should design balanced reward systems focusing on knowledge retention rather than mere engagement. Transparent goals and opt-out options promote ethical use of gamified features.

41. Discuss how you would implement WebRTC for peer-to-peer video calls in a web application.
Answer: WebRTC enables direct browser-to-browser communication without servers for media relay. MCA graduates should handle signaling through WebSockets, manage NAT traversal using STUN/TURN servers, and encrypt streams with SRTP for privacy.

42. Explain how to secure a multi-tenant database architecture in a SaaS application.
Answer: Multi-tenant databases risk data leaks between tenants. MCA graduates should enforce tenant isolation using row-level security, tenant-specific encryption keys, and thorough access control mechanisms. Regular audits and penetration tests ensure data segregation integrity.

43. Analyze how to design an API for IoT devices with limited processing power.
Answer: IoT APIs must be lightweight and efficient. MCA graduates should use concise data formats like Protocol Buffers instead of JSON and design stateless APIs for reduced overhead. Implementing secure, token-based authentication balances performance with security.

44. Discuss how to integrate real-time analytics in a web-based stock trading platform.
Answer: Real-time analytics require low latency and high throughput. MCA graduates should use WebSockets for live data feeds and in-memory databases like Redis for fast computations. Data visualization libraries render insights instantly, supporting quick trading decisions.

45. Explain the role of ethical data collection in fitness tracking web applications.
Answer: Fitness apps collect sensitive health data. MCA graduates should anonymize and encrypt data, obtain informed user consent, and avoid sharing with third parties without permission. Clear privacy policies and opt-out features ensure ethical compliance.

46. Analyze how browser push notifications enhance user engagement in e-commerce apps.
Answer: Push notifications re-engage users with personalized updates on offers or order statuses. MCA graduates should design opt-in flows, allow granular notification preferences, and avoid spamming to maintain user trust and compliance with privacy laws.

47. Discuss how you would implement file upload validation to prevent malware in a web app.
Answer: Validating file uploads involves restricting allowed types, scanning for viruses, and limiting file sizes. MCA graduates should use server-side checks and store files in non-executable directories to prevent malicious code execution.

48. Explain how to design a multilingual PWA for global audiences.
Answer: MCA graduates should use internationalization (i18n) frameworks, language-specific content caching, and detect browser locale settings for default language selection. Providing manual language switches ensures accessibility across diverse user bases.

49. Analyze how to secure cookies in web applications against session hijacking.
Answer: MCA graduates should set cookies with the Secure and HttpOnly flags to prevent transmission over HTTP and client-side access via JavaScript. Using SameSite attributes protects against CSRF, and session expiration policies mitigate hijacking risks.

50. Discuss how ethical considerations influence targeted advertising in children's web platforms.
Answer: Targeted ads for children can exploit vulnerabilities. MCA graduates should comply with regulations like COPPA, avoid collecting unnecessary data, and prioritize educational or age-appropriate content in ad placements to maintain ethical standards.

51. Explain how to design a secure REST API for a healthcare management system.
Answer: REST APIs in healthcare handle sensitive data, requiring strict security measures. MCA graduates should implement HTTPS for encrypted data transmission, use OAuth 2.0 for secure authorization, and validate all incoming requests. Input sanitization prevents injection attacks, while rate limiting protects against brute-force attempts. Storing minimal patient data and ensuring compliance with HIPAA or GDPR regulations enhances security and user trust.

52. Discuss the role of ethical user data handling in e-learning platforms.
Answer: E-learning platforms often collect personal and academic data, raising privacy concerns. MCA graduates should anonymize data where possible, obtain explicit consent for data collection, and allow users to control their

information. Ethical handling includes using data solely for educational purposes and securing it against breaches, ensuring trust among students and institutions.

53. Analyze how to optimize a single-page application (SPA) for fast initial load times.
Answer: SPAs often suffer from heavy initial downloads. MCA graduates should implement code splitting, lazy load non-critical components, and prefetch essential data. Using server-side rendering (SSR) or static site generation (SSG) can speed up the first paint, improving perceived performance for users.

54. Explain how to integrate third-party APIs securely in web applications.
Answer: Third-party APIs can introduce vulnerabilities if not properly handled. MCA graduates should use API keys or OAuth for authentication, restrict API scopes to the minimum necessary, and validate API responses before processing. Rate limiting and monitoring API usage ensure stability and protect against misuse.

55. Discuss how Progressive Web Apps (PWAs) improve user engagement for retail businesses.
Answer: PWAs combine the reach of the web with app-like experiences, enabling offline browsing, push notifications, and faster load times. MCA graduates should design PWAs for retail businesses to increase user retention and conversions by offering seamless shopping experiences on all devices without requiring app downloads.

56. Explain how to implement secure password reset functionality in web applications.
Answer: Secure password resets require generating time-bound, random tokens sent via email or SMS. MCA graduates should store tokens hashed in the database, verify their validity before allowing resets, and enforce strong new password policies. Limiting reset attempts and notifying users of changes further strengthens security.

57. Analyze how web developers can use browser local storage without compromising security.
Answer: Local storage offers convenient client-side data persistence but is vulnerable to XSS attacks. MCA graduates should avoid storing sensitive data like tokens and encrypt non-sensitive information when needed. Regular input sanitization and setting a Content Security Policy (CSP) help reduce risks.

58. Discuss how to design a secure file download system in a document management portal.
Answer: To secure downloads, MCA graduates should validate user permissions before serving files, use temporary signed URLs, and scan files for malware before upload. Implementing rate limiting and logging download activities prevents abuse and ensures accountability.

59. Explain how Content Delivery Networks (CDNs) enhance scalability for global web applications.
Answer: CDNs distribute static assets across edge servers worldwide, enabling users to fetch resources from nearby locations, reducing latency. MCA graduates should configure CDNs for caching images, scripts, and videos, ensuring web apps scale effectively under high global traffic.

60. Discuss the ethical use of cookies in personalization features of web platforms.
Answer: Cookies enable personalized experiences but may infringe on user privacy. MCA graduates should use cookies transparently, obtain consent through cookie banners, and avoid unnecessary tracking. Providing clear options for users to manage their preferences aligns with ethical standards and data privacy laws like GDPR.

61. Analyze how WebSockets support real-time multiplayer gaming applications.
Answer: WebSockets maintain persistent connections, enabling instant updates for all connected players. MCA graduates should handle concurrency issues, implement encryption (WSS), and design efficient data structures to reduce latency and packet loss for smooth gameplay.

62. Explain how to prevent cross-origin resource sharing (CORS) misconfigurations in APIs.
Answer: Improper CORS configurations expose APIs to unauthorized access. MCA graduates should explicitly define allowed origins, methods, and headers in server responses. Avoid using wildcard * for sensitive endpoints and implement preflight request validation to strengthen API security.

63. Discuss how web accessibility benefits businesses and users alike.

Answer: Accessible websites cater to a broader audience, including people with disabilities, improving inclusivity and compliance with laws like ADA. MCA graduates should design with semantic HTML, ARIA roles, and color-contrast guidelines, enhancing usability and reaching more customers.

64. Explain how to secure GraphQL APIs against over-fetching and denial-of-service attacks.
Answer: GraphQL APIs allow clients to specify data needs, but malicious queries can overload servers. MCA graduates should implement query depth limiting, throttling, and whitelisting of operations. Validating inputs and using persisted queries further strengthen GraphQL security.

65. Analyze how web developers can design ethical nudges in user interfaces.
Answer: Nudges encourage desired actions but risk manipulating users. MCA graduates should design nudges that respect autonomy, such as gentle reminders for incomplete profiles rather than dark patterns. Transparency and user control make nudges ethical and effective.

66. Discuss how to optimize an image-heavy portfolio website for performance.
Answer: MCA graduates should use responsive images (`srcset`), next-gen formats like WebP, and lazy loading to reduce initial load time. Implementing image compression and CDN caching ensures a visually rich yet performant website for creative professionals.

67. Explain how web workers improve performance in computationally intensive web applications.
Answer: Web workers offload heavy JavaScript tasks from the main thread, preventing UI blocking. MCA graduates should use them for background operations like data parsing or image processing to keep applications responsive.

68. Analyze the security concerns of storing API keys in front-end code.
Answer: Storing API keys client-side exposes them to attackers through browser developer tools. MCA graduates should proxy API calls through back-end servers or use environment variables to keep keys confidential.

69. Discuss how service workers enhance offline capabilities in travel booking applications.
Answer: Service workers cache essential resources like itineraries and booking details, enabling offline access. MCA graduates should design caching strategies to balance freshness and performance, ensuring smooth user experiences even in areas with poor connectivity.

70. Explain how to implement rate limiting for public APIs in a weather forecasting web app.
Answer: Rate limiting prevents excessive requests from overloading servers. MCA graduates should set thresholds based on IP or API keys, return `429 Too Many Requests` responses, and provide developers with clear usage policies and upgrade options.

71. Analyze the ethical considerations of using heatmaps in web analytics.
Answer: Heatmaps show user interaction patterns but may capture sensitive data. MCA graduates should anonymize data, avoid logging form inputs, and obtain user consent to ensure ethical analytics practices.

72. Discuss how to secure multi-step forms in web applications.
Answer: Multi-step forms should validate data at each stage to prevent injection attacks. MCA graduates should use CSRF tokens, secure HTTPS connections, and store partial progress on the server to prevent tampering.

73. Explain how GraphQL differs from REST and its use in building dashboards.
Answer: GraphQL enables clients to fetch specific data in a single request, reducing over-fetching common in REST APIs. MCA graduates should use GraphQL to power dashboards requiring flexible, dynamic data visualization with minimal server requests.

74. Analyze how web developers can design user-centric interfaces for government service portals.
Answer: Government portals serve diverse users, including those with limited digital literacy. MCA graduates should prioritize clarity, use simple language, and design responsive layouts with accessibility in mind, ensuring inclusivity for all citizens.

75. Discuss the importance of logging and monitoring in maintaining secure web applications.

Answer: Logging tracks application events, and monitoring detects anomalies in real-time. MCA graduates should implement centralized logging systems and use alerting tools to identify and respond to security incidents quickly, minimizing potential damage.

76. Explain how to design a secure multi-factor authentication (MFA) system for online banking portals.
Answer: Multi-factor authentication enhances security by requiring multiple verification methods. MCA graduates should integrate something the user knows (password), something they have (OTP via SMS/email or authenticator app), and something they are (biometrics). Tokens must be time-bound and encrypted during transmission. Backup codes and device recognition can improve usability while maintaining security. Proper implementation of MFA mitigates risks like credential theft and phishing.

77. Discuss how web developers can optimize web applications for users on low-end devices.
Answer: Optimizing for low-end devices involves reducing resource consumption and ensuring lightweight designs. MCA graduates should use progressive enhancement, limit JavaScript dependencies, and compress images and scripts. Techniques like adaptive loading and server-side rendering improve performance, ensuring smooth operation even on devices with limited processing power and memory.

78. Analyze the ethical challenges of using machine learning for content recommendation in news websites.
Answer: Machine learning-driven recommendations can create echo chambers and spread misinformation. MCA graduates must ensure algorithmic transparency, avoid reinforcing biases, and provide users with options to customize or turn off recommendations. Balancing personalization with exposure to diverse perspectives promotes ethical and responsible content delivery.

79. Explain how to implement secure API authentication using OAuth 2.0 in social media platforms.
Answer: OAuth 2.0 allows users to grant limited access to their data without sharing passwords. MCA graduates should implement authorization code flow for web apps, securely store access tokens, and refresh them periodically. Using scopes restricts API access to necessary permissions, while HTTPS ensures safe transmission of sensitive data.

80. Discuss how to design a scalable architecture for a live streaming platform.
Answer: Live streaming requires low latency and high scalability. MCA graduates should use distributed servers, CDNs for video delivery, and adaptive bitrate streaming to handle variable network conditions. Load balancers and microservices architecture ensure the system can handle millions of concurrent users while maintaining quality.

81. Analyze how to protect sensitive customer data in e-commerce web applications.
Answer: Protecting customer data requires encryption in transit (HTTPS) and at rest (AES). MCA graduates should implement secure password hashing (bcrypt), use tokenized payment systems, and minimize data collection to only essential details. Regular security audits and compliance with standards like PCI DSS ensure data protection and build customer trust.

82. Explain how service workers improve caching strategies for Progressive Web Apps (PWAs).
Answer: Service workers act as intermediaries between the browser and server, enabling advanced caching. MCA graduates should use precaching for critical resources and runtime caching for dynamic content. Cache versioning ensures users receive updated assets, while fallback pages provide seamless offline experiences.

83. Discuss how ethical considerations influence the design of push notifications in web apps.
Answer: Push notifications can enhance engagement but may irritate users if overused. MCA graduates should design opt-in mechanisms, allow users to control notification frequency, and avoid sending intrusive or irrelevant content. Ethical use ensures user trust and prevents app abandonment.

84. Explain how to prevent clickjacking attacks in financial web applications.
Answer: Clickjacking tricks users into performing unintended actions. MCA graduates should set the `X-Frame-Options` header to `DENY` or `SAMEORIGIN` and use Content Security Policy (CSP) frame-ancestors directive. These measures prevent the app from being embedded in iframes on malicious sites.

85. Discuss how to design a multilingual web application supporting right-to-left (RTL) languages.

Answer: Multilingual apps require dynamic language switching and layout adjustments for RTL languages like Arabic. MCA graduates should use i18n frameworks, CSS logical properties (e.g., `margin-inline-start`), and test designs thoroughly to ensure proper alignment and readability across all supported languages.

86. Analyze the benefits and challenges of using micro-frontends in large-scale web projects.
Answer: Micro-frontends break UI into independent, reusable modules, improving scalability and team productivity. MCA graduates should manage shared dependencies carefully to avoid duplication and ensure smooth integration. While micro-frontends enable faster development, they can introduce complexity in deployment and state management.

87. Explain how to design a secure logout mechanism in web applications.
Answer: Secure logout ensures all user sessions are terminated properly. MCA graduates should clear session tokens, invalidate JWTs on the server side, and redirect users to a confirmation page. Using short session lifetimes and monitoring token reuse prevents session hijacking.

88. Discuss how to handle large file uploads efficiently in web applications.
Answer: Large file uploads can strain servers and networks. MCA graduates should implement chunked uploads, resumable upload APIs, and background processing queues. Validating file size and type on the server ensures security, while progress indicators improve user experience.

89. Analyze how to prevent replay attacks in web APIs.
Answer: Replay attacks involve resending valid requests maliciously. MCA graduates should implement nonce values and timestamp validation to ensure requests are unique and time-bound. HTTPS encryption and short-lived tokens further reduce risks.

90. Explain how to optimize critical rendering paths in responsive web applications.
Answer: Optimizing the critical rendering path reduces load times. MCA graduates should minimize CSS blocking resources, defer non-critical JavaScript, and inline critical CSS for faster initial rendering. These practices improve metrics like First Contentful Paint (FCP).

91. Discuss how ethical design impacts user trust in subscription-based web platforms.
Answer: Ethical design avoids dark patterns like hidden fees or difficult cancellations. MCA graduates should ensure transparent pricing, easy subscription management, and clear communication about trial periods. Ethical practices build long-term trust and customer loyalty.

92. Explain how to secure WebSocket communication in real-time chat applications.
Answer: WebSockets require encryption (WSS) to protect data in transit. MCA graduates should implement authentication mechanisms like tokens during the handshake, validate incoming messages, and set limits to prevent denial-of-service (DoS) attacks.

93. Analyze how web developers can use lazy loading to improve page performance.
Answer: Lazy loading defers the loading of images or scripts until they are needed. MCA graduates should use `loading="lazy"` for images and dynamic imports for JavaScript modules, reducing initial page load times and conserving bandwidth.

94. Discuss how to design an API that supports versioning for future scalability.
Answer: API versioning allows backward compatibility as APIs evolve. MCA graduates should use version identifiers in URLs (e.g., `/v1/`) or headers, documenting changes clearly to avoid breaking existing client integrations.

95. Explain the role of web accessibility standards (WCAG) in government websites.
Answer: WCAG ensures websites are usable by people with disabilities. MCA graduates should design keyboard-navigable interfaces, provide alt text for images, and ensure sufficient color contrast, meeting legal and ethical accessibility requirements.

96. Discuss how to handle user authentication in single-page applications (SPAs).

Answer: SPAs require secure token-based authentication. MCA graduates should store tokens in HTTP-only cookies to prevent XSS attacks and refresh them periodically using silent authentication techniques. Validating tokens on every API call ensures secure access.

97. Analyze the challenges of implementing server-side rendering (SSR) in React applications.
Answer: SSR improves SEO and initial load speed but introduces complexity in managing state and third-party libraries. MCA graduates should use frameworks like Next.js to simplify SSR and handle challenges like hydration errors efficiently.

98. Explain how to design a real-time notification system for collaboration tools.
Answer: Real-time notifications require persistent connections using WebSockets or push APIs. MCA graduates should design backend systems that broadcast events efficiently and implement user preferences to control notification types and frequencies.

99. Discuss how to secure cloud-hosted web applications against data breaches.
Answer: MCA graduates should enforce encryption at rest and in transit, use identity and access management (IAM) controls, and regularly audit permissions. Implementing firewalls and intrusion detection systems protects applications against external threats.

100. Explain the ethical considerations of using behavioral analytics in web applications.
Answer: Behavioral analytics provide insights into user interactions but can invade privacy. MCA graduates should anonymize data, seek user consent, and allow opt-out options. Ethical analytics practices balance insights with respect for user rights.

101. Explain how to implement a secure session management system in a SaaS web application.
Answer: Secure session management ensures user authentication remains robust throughout a session. MCA graduates should use HTTPS to encrypt session data in transit and store session identifiers securely in HTTP-only cookies to prevent XSS attacks. Regenerating session IDs on login and logout prevents fixation attacks, while implementing idle timeouts and absolute expiration limits further enhances security. Server-side session storage should use encrypted databases with strict access controls.

102. Discuss how ethical UI design prevents dark patterns in e-commerce platforms.
Answer: Dark patterns mislead users into unwanted actions like subscribing or overspending. MCA graduates should avoid hidden opt-outs, pre-selected checkboxes, and confusing layouts. Transparent pricing, clear consent prompts, and undo options foster trust and ethical user experiences, enhancing customer loyalty in e-commerce platforms.

103. Analyze the importance of implementing role-based access control (RBAC) in enterprise web applications.
Answer: RBAC restricts user actions based on assigned roles, preventing unauthorized access to sensitive features. MCA graduates should design granular permissions, enforce least privilege principles, and log access attempts for auditing. Implementing RBAC ensures security, compliance, and operational efficiency in multi-user enterprise systems.

104. Explain how to design an offline-first architecture for a job search web application.
Answer: Offline-first designs enhance usability in low-connectivity areas. MCA graduates should use service workers to cache critical resources, IndexedDB for storing user activity, and background synchronization for updating data when online. This approach ensures job seekers can browse postings and save applications seamlessly, even offline.

105. Discuss the challenges of implementing GDPR compliance in data-heavy web portals.
Answer: GDPR compliance requires data minimization, explicit consent, and user rights for data access and deletion. MCA graduates should design portals with consent management tools, encryption mechanisms, and audit logs. Implementing anonymization for analytics data balances privacy with functionality in data-heavy systems.

106. Explain how to secure API integrations in financial web applications.

Answer: APIs in financial apps handle sensitive transactions, requiring robust security. MCA graduates should use OAuth 2.0 or JWT for authentication, validate inputs to prevent injection attacks, and enable HTTPS for encrypted communication. Rate limiting, IP whitelisting, and constant monitoring help detect and mitigate potential abuse.

107. Discuss how to implement real-time collaboration features in web-based project management tools.
Answer: Real-time collaboration requires instant updates across users. MCA graduates should use WebSockets or technologies like Firebase for live syncing and conflict resolution algorithms like CRDTs. Proper user authentication and data consistency checks prevent unauthorized access and data corruption.

108. Analyze how to design a secure password storage mechanism for a social networking platform.
Answer: Passwords must never be stored in plaintext. MCA graduates should hash passwords using algorithms like bcrypt or Argon2 with unique salts for each user. Limiting login attempts and enabling MFA strengthens security, while regular security audits detect vulnerabilities proactively.

109. Explain how microservices architecture improves scalability in large web applications.
Answer: Microservices divide applications into smaller, independent services, enabling horizontal scaling and focused deployments. MCA graduates should design APIs for inter-service communication and use containerization tools like Docker and Kubernetes to manage scalability and reliability in production environments.

110. Discuss the ethical implications of collecting user location data in ride-hailing web apps.
Answer: Location data is sensitive and prone to misuse. MCA graduates should obtain informed consent, anonymize data for analytics, and provide granular privacy controls. Adhering to data protection laws like GDPR ensures ethical handling and fosters user trust in ride-hailing services.

111. Explain how to secure third-party JavaScript libraries in web development.
Answer: Third-party libraries can introduce vulnerabilities if outdated or compromised. MCA graduates should use Subresource Integrity (SRI) hashes to verify script authenticity, audit dependencies regularly, and prefer libraries from trusted sources. Bundling only required components minimizes potential attack surfaces.

112. Discuss how to design a secure RESTful API for IoT devices in smart homes.
Answer: REST APIs for IoT must prioritize security due to device constraints and privacy concerns. MCA graduates should implement lightweight authentication (e.g., token-based), encrypt all traffic with HTTPS, and use whitelisted IPs. Rate limiting prevents DDoS attacks on resource-constrained devices.

113. Analyze how content personalization impacts user engagement in e-learning platforms.
Answer: Personalization tailors content to user preferences, improving engagement and retention. MCA graduates should use algorithms that recommend courses or resources while respecting privacy. Offering opt-out options and transparent data usage policies ensures personalization remains ethical and user-centric.

114. Explain how to design a secure file sharing system for enterprise collaboration platforms.
Answer: Secure file sharing requires encrypted storage and transmission. MCA graduates should implement role-based permissions, virus scanning on uploads, and activity logs for auditing. Time-limited and access-controlled download links prevent unauthorized sharing outside the organization.

115. Discuss how to prevent XSS and CSRF attacks in web-based CRM applications.
Answer: XSS prevention involves sanitizing and encoding user inputs, while CSRF protection uses anti-CSRF tokens and SameSite cookie attributes. MCA graduates should combine these measures with regular security testing to safeguard CRM systems handling sensitive client data.

116. Explain how to optimize server response times in high-traffic web applications.
Answer: Optimizing server response involves caching frequently accessed data, using load balancers, and optimizing database queries. MCA graduates should employ asynchronous processing for long-running tasks and use CDN edge caching to reduce server load during traffic spikes.

117. Discuss the role of ethical considerations in designing persuasive interfaces for fitness apps.

Answer: Persuasive interfaces can motivate but may also manipulate user behavior. MCA graduates should design with transparency, avoid unhealthy competition or guilt-inducing features, and prioritize user well-being over engagement metrics.

118. Analyze how HTTPS ensures data confidentiality and integrity in web applications.
Answer: HTTPS uses SSL/TLS protocols to encrypt data during transit, preventing eavesdropping and tampering. MCA graduates should enforce HTTPS across all pages, configure HSTS headers, and use strong certificates to ensure secure communication between clients and servers.

119. Explain how to implement a real-time voting system for virtual events.
Answer: Real-time voting requires efficient data handling and instant updates. MCA graduates should use WebSockets for bi-directional communication, store votes in an in-memory database for speed, and ensure data integrity with secure APIs and encryption.

120. Discuss how to secure REST APIs exposed to third-party developers.
Answer: Public APIs require authentication (OAuth 2.0), API key management, and rate limiting to prevent misuse. MCA graduates should validate incoming data, enforce HTTPS, and use API gateways with monitoring and logging features to secure access.

121. Explain the importance of ethical AI use in chatbots for customer support.
Answer: AI chatbots improve efficiency but risk spreading misinformation or bias. MCA graduates should train bots on diverse datasets, involve human review for escalations, and disclose when users are interacting with AI to ensure ethical and transparent communication.

122. Discuss how to optimize front-end performance in a feature-rich dashboard application.
Answer: Front-end optimization involves code splitting, lazy loading, and minimizing DOM manipulations. MCA graduates should use virtual scrolling for large datasets, compress assets, and apply tree-shaking to remove unused code, ensuring a smooth dashboard experience.

123. Analyze how to design an API gateway to manage multiple microservices securely.
Answer: API gateways centralize traffic and security management. MCA graduates should implement authentication, request throttling, and SSL termination. Logging and anomaly detection at the gateway level helps secure communication between clients and microservices.

124. Explain how to implement secure data synchronization in collaborative editing tools.
Answer: Data synchronization requires conflict resolution and secure transmission. MCA graduates should use algorithms like Operational Transformation (OT), encrypt data during sync, and authenticate clients to prevent unauthorized changes in collaborative environments.

125. Discuss the ethical responsibilities of web developers when designing persuasive UX in mental health apps.
Answer: Persuasive UX in mental health apps must avoid exploiting users' emotional states. MCA graduates should design with empathy, provide clear disclaimers, and ensure features promote user well-being over engagement or monetization goals. Transparency and ethical testing with target audiences are essential.

126. Explain how to secure third-party integrations in payment systems for web applications.
Answer: Third-party payment systems handle sensitive financial data and must be secured rigorously. MCA graduates should validate API endpoints, use secure OAuth tokens for authentication, and limit permissions to only essential scopes. Implementing HTTPS, regular API key rotation, and webhook validation ensures secure communication. Logging and monitoring API activity also help detect suspicious behavior early, safeguarding both users and merchants.

127. Discuss how to design a real-time ride-tracking system for a cab booking web app.
Answer: A ride-tracking system uses GPS and real-time updates to display driver locations. MCA graduates should leverage WebSockets or MQTT for efficient bi-directional communication and implement map APIs like Google

Maps for visualization. Optimizing updates for low-latency while conserving bandwidth ensures smooth tracking, and strong encryption protects user location data.

128. Analyze how to handle data privacy in a web application offering personalized health recommendations.
Answer: Health apps process sensitive personal data. MCA graduates should implement explicit consent mechanisms, anonymize health records for analytics, and encrypt data in transit and storage. Ensuring compliance with regulations like HIPAA or GDPR is critical. Privacy dashboards allow users to control and delete their data, reinforcing ethical practices.

129. Explain how to design a highly available architecture for a stock trading web platform.
Answer: Stock trading platforms demand zero downtime and fast execution. MCA graduates should implement load balancing, database replication, and failover mechanisms to achieve high availability. Distributed caching and real-time monitoring tools like Prometheus ensure consistent performance, even during peak trading hours.

130. Discuss how to prevent privilege escalation in admin panels of web applications.
Answer: Privilege escalation occurs when lower-privileged users gain unauthorized access to admin features. MCA graduates should enforce strict role-based access controls (RBAC), validate server-side permissions for every action, and audit logs regularly. Using multi-factor authentication (MFA) for admin accounts adds an extra layer of protection.

131. Explain how to use GraphQL subscriptions for real-time updates in collaboration tools.
Answer: GraphQL subscriptions allow clients to receive real-time data through WebSockets. MCA graduates should design secure resolvers to handle subscription events like document edits or comments. Optimizing backend data sources ensures efficient broadcasting without overloading servers.

132. Discuss how ethical design can prevent addiction in social media platforms.
Answer: Social media apps often exploit psychological triggers to increase engagement. MCA graduates should avoid infinite scroll, excessive notifications, and manipulative algorithms. Features like usage limits and well-being reminders promote healthy user habits and align with ethical development practices.

133. Analyze how browser sandboxing enhances security for embedded third-party scripts.
Answer: Sandboxing restricts what third-party scripts can do in the browser. MCA graduates should use the `<iframe>` sandbox attribute to isolate scripts, limiting access to cookies and local storage. Content Security Policy (CSP) headers further reduce risks by restricting external resource loading.

134. Explain how to optimize content-heavy e-learning platforms for users with limited bandwidth.
Answer: MCA graduates should implement adaptive streaming for videos, use image compression, and leverage CDNs for static content delivery. Offline access via service workers and preloading essential resources ensures usability in bandwidth-constrained environments.

135. Discuss how to secure webhooks in payment and logistics systems.
Answer: Webhooks notify systems of events but can be exploited if unsecured. MCA graduates should verify webhook signatures using shared secrets or public key cryptography. IP whitelisting and HTTPS encryption prevent interception and tampering during data transmission.

136. Explain how AI chatbots in web applications can maintain user privacy.
Answer: AI chatbots handle personal user data, so MCA graduates should anonymize inputs and avoid storing sensitive information unless necessary. Transparent privacy notices and secure API integrations with backend systems ensure responsible handling of user conversations.

137. Analyze how to design a decentralized web application (dApp) using blockchain technology.
Answer: dApps store data and transactions on distributed ledgers. MCA graduates should design smart contracts carefully to prevent vulnerabilities and use blockchain networks like Ethereum for decentralization. Decentralized storage (IPFS) ensures redundancy and censorship resistance.

138. Discuss how ethical considerations apply to dynamic pricing algorithms in e-commerce websites.

Answer: Dynamic pricing adjusts costs based on demand but risks price discrimination. MCA graduates should ensure transparency, avoid unfair targeting of vulnerable groups, and comply with consumer protection laws to maintain ethical standards.

139. Explain how to secure REST APIs in multi-tenant SaaS applications.
Answer: Multi-tenant SaaS APIs must isolate tenant data securely. MCA graduates should enforce tenant-aware authorization, validate all incoming data, and encrypt sensitive information. Using API gateways with throttling helps maintain stability under multi-tenant loads.

140. Discuss how to design a real-time auction platform with high concurrency.
Answer: Real-time auctions require low-latency updates and concurrency control. MCA graduates should use WebSockets for bid updates, distributed databases for scalability, and queuing systems to manage simultaneous bids reliably.

141. Explain how to prevent session fixation attacks in user authentication flows.
Answer: MCA graduates should regenerate session IDs after user authentication and avoid using URL parameters for session tracking. Implementing strict cookie attributes (HttpOnly, Secure, SameSite) and short-lived tokens further mitigates fixation risks.

142. Analyze how ethical UX principles improve trust in charity fundraising web platforms.
Answer: Ethical UX focuses on clarity, avoiding manipulative donation flows or guilt-based messaging. MCA graduates should design transparent progress indicators, clear donation terms, and opt-in choices for recurring contributions, building donor trust.

143. Discuss how to optimize web apps for foldable and dual-screen devices.
Answer: Foldable devices require adaptive layouts. MCA graduates should use media queries for multi-screen scenarios, test split-screen behaviors, and design flexible UIs that adjust seamlessly across screen configurations.

144. Explain how web developers can secure API keys in client-side applications.
Answer: API keys in front-end code can be exposed through browser tools. MCA graduates should proxy API requests through secure backends, rotate keys regularly, and limit their scope to reduce potential abuse.

145. Discuss how to implement secure payment flows using tokenization in e-commerce platforms.
Answer: Tokenization replaces sensitive card details with unique tokens for transactions. MCA graduates should integrate with PCI DSS-compliant providers and avoid storing raw payment data on their servers, reducing exposure to breaches.

146. Explain how to design a secure Single Sign-On (SSO) system for enterprise web applications.
Answer: Single Sign-On allows users to access multiple applications with one set of credentials. MCA graduates should implement protocols like SAML or OAuth 2.0 and ensure encrypted token exchanges. Verifying the authenticity of identity providers and applying strong session management practices prevents token misuse. Multi-factor authentication (MFA) can further strengthen security, especially in enterprise environments where data sensitivity is high.

147. Discuss how to optimize Progressive Web Apps (PWAs) for low-power devices.
Answer: PWAs on low-power devices must minimize resource consumption. MCA graduates should use lightweight frameworks, lazy load resources, and compress assets. Limiting background processes and optimizing service workers for caching critical data only helps reduce battery and memory drain, ensuring better performance on entry-level devices.

148. Analyze how to prevent data leaks in web-based healthcare portals.
Answer: Healthcare portals store sensitive personal health information (PHI). MCA graduates should encrypt data at rest and in transit, use strict access controls, and perform regular security audits. Implementing audit trails for all access events and adhering to HIPAA or GDPR compliance ensures sensitive health data is protected.

149. Explain how ethical UI design avoids manipulative patterns in subscription-based services.

Answer: Ethical UI prevents users from being misled into purchases. MCA graduates should avoid pre-checked boxes for subscriptions, make cancellation options visible, and ensure transparent pricing. This approach builds long-term trust with users instead of relying on deceptive practices to boost short-term revenue.

150. Discuss how to secure APIs that are consumed by mobile applications.
Answer: Mobile APIs are often targeted by attackers. MCA graduates should use token-based authentication (OAuth 2.0 or JWT), validate all inputs, and enable HTTPS for encrypted data transmission. Adding device fingerprinting and implementing API rate limiting protects against misuse.

151. Explain how to design a real-time inventory management system for retail web applications.
Answer: Real-time inventory requires continuous synchronization across multiple endpoints. MCA graduates should use WebSockets for live updates, implement distributed databases for scalability, and apply optimistic locking to prevent conflicts during concurrent stock updates.

152. Analyze the ethical considerations of tracking user interactions in productivity web apps.
Answer: Tracking interactions helps improve UX but raises privacy concerns. MCA graduates should anonymize data, notify users about tracking, and allow them to opt out. Transparent policies ensure user trust and compliance with data protection regulations.

153. Discuss how to optimize database queries for high-performance web APIs.
Answer: MCA graduates should use indexing, caching frequently queried data, and optimizing joins to reduce response times. Avoiding N+1 query issues and using connection pooling in high-traffic environments ensures APIs remain performant under load.

154. Explain how to secure cloud-hosted web applications from insider threats.
Answer: Insider threats are often overlooked. MCA graduates should enforce least privilege access, use role-based access controls, and enable logging of all sensitive operations. Multi-factor authentication for administrative accounts and regular audits detect and prevent unauthorized actions.

155. Discuss how to implement secure file upload functionality for user-generated content websites.
Answer: Secure file uploads require validation on the server side. MCA graduates should restrict allowed file types, limit file sizes, scan uploads for malware, and store files in non-executable directories. Using signed URLs for file access further prevents unauthorized sharing.

156. Explain how to design ethical reward systems in web-based gamification platforms.
Answer: Ethical reward systems encourage participation without manipulation. MCA graduates should avoid addictive patterns and ensure rewards promote learning or productivity. Giving users the choice to engage and setting clear expectations builds a healthier user experience.

157. Analyze how to prevent race conditions in collaborative real-time applications.
Answer: Race conditions occur when simultaneous operations cause inconsistent states. MCA graduates should implement server-side conflict resolution strategies like locking, use CRDTs for eventual consistency, and carefully handle asynchronous operations to prevent data corruption.

158. Discuss how WebAssembly enhances computational performance in browser-based applications.
Answer: WebAssembly runs low-level code (e.g., C/C++) in the browser at near-native speeds. MCA graduates should use it for CPU-intensive tasks like 3D rendering or encryption. Integrating WebAssembly with JavaScript allows for efficient hybrid applications.

159. Explain how to secure cross-origin communication in web applications using CORS policies.
Answer: Cross-origin requests need careful handling to avoid vulnerabilities. MCA graduates should define explicit origins in CORS headers, avoid wildcard * for sensitive endpoints, and validate preflight requests. Using secure tokens and HTTPS ensures safe cross-origin data sharing.

160. Discuss how to design a scalable architecture for a multi-tenant SaaS web application.

Answer: Multi-tenant SaaS apps serve multiple clients on shared infrastructure. MCA graduates should design tenant-aware databases using row-level security or separate schemas, implement API rate limiting, and use container orchestration (e.g., Kubernetes) for scaling services efficiently.

161. Explain how to prevent XSS attacks in Single Page Applications (SPAs).
Answer: SPAs rely heavily on client-side JavaScript, making XSS prevention critical. MCA graduates should sanitize all user inputs, use secure frameworks that auto-escape outputs (like React), and implement Content Security Policies (CSP) to block inline scripts.

162. Analyze the ethical implications of algorithmic bias in AI-driven recruitment platforms.
Answer: AI recruitment tools risk reinforcing societal biases. MCA graduates should audit algorithms regularly, ensure diverse and representative training datasets, and provide transparency in decision-making to promote fairness and inclusivity.

163. Discuss how service workers enable background sync in Progressive Web Apps.
Answer: Background sync allows PWAs to queue user actions offline and send them when connectivity resumes. MCA graduates should use service workers and the Background Sync API to enhance reliability, ensuring users' actions are preserved seamlessly.

164. Explain how to secure web applications against SQL injection attacks.
Answer: SQL injection exploits unsanitized inputs. MCA graduates should use parameterized queries, ORM frameworks, and input validation to prevent malicious SQL code execution. Limiting database privileges further reduces risks.

165. Discuss how ethical practices in data collection improve trust in fitness tracking apps.
Answer: Fitness apps gather sensitive health and activity data. MCA graduates should provide clear consent forms, anonymize datasets for analytics, and allow users to delete their data. Ethical practices enhance brand trust and user retention.

166. Explain how to implement content moderation in user-generated content web platforms.
Answer: Content moderation prevents harmful or inappropriate content. MCA graduates should combine automated filters (e.g., AI classifiers) with human review for edge cases. Transparent moderation policies and appeal mechanisms ensure fairness.

167. Analyze how to design a secure voting system for online polls.
Answer: Secure voting requires protecting vote integrity and user anonymity. MCA graduates should use encrypted channels, validate user identities, and prevent duplicate submissions using token-based authentication. Audit logs help ensure transparency.

168. Discuss how to optimize web applications for voice search compatibility.
Answer: Voice search requires semantic HTML, structured data (Schema.org), and fast-loading pages. MCA graduates should ensure natural language support in APIs and prioritize mobile-first design for voice-based user interactions.

169. Explain how to secure WebSocket connections in browser-based multiplayer games.
Answer: Secure WebSocket (WSS) ensures encrypted communication. MCA graduates should authenticate clients during handshakes, validate messages server-side, and implement rate limiting to prevent flooding or denial-of-service (DoS) attacks.

170. Discuss the ethical considerations of using gamification in e-learning platforms for children.
Answer: Gamification boosts engagement but may foster addictive behaviors in children. MCA graduates should design age-appropriate reward systems, avoid dark patterns, and focus on educational outcomes over continuous engagement.

171. Explain how to implement secure data synchronization in web apps using IndexedDB.

Answer: IndexedDB stores offline data in browsers. MCA graduates should encrypt sensitive data, manage versioning carefully during sync, and resolve conflicts with timestamps or server validation to ensure consistent updates.

172. Analyze how to prevent phishing attacks in web-based email clients.
Answer: MCA graduates should detect and warn users about suspicious links using URL filtering and DNS-based blacklists. Enforcing HTTPS, validating sender authenticity with SPF/DKIM/DMARC, and educating users about phishing signs strengthen security.

173. Discuss how to optimize REST APIs for mobile applications with limited bandwidth.
Answer: Optimizing REST APIs involves compressing responses (GZIP), implementing pagination, and reducing payload size with selective field queries. MCA graduates should use caching mechanisms and support offline capabilities where feasible.

174. Explain how to secure user-uploaded media in social networking web apps.
Answer: User uploads can introduce malware or expose private data. MCA graduates should scan files for viruses, store them in non-public directories, and use signed URLs for temporary access. Enforcing content size limits also helps manage storage.

175. Discuss how ethical AI transparency builds trust in customer-facing web chatbots.
Answer: Transparency about AI use helps users understand they're interacting with a machine. MCA graduates should provide disclaimers, allow users to request human support, and avoid opaque decision-making. This fosters trust and mitigates concerns about bias or misinformation.

176. Explain how to design a secure passwordless authentication system for web applications.
Answer: Passwordless authentication enhances security by replacing traditional passwords with one-time codes or magic links. MCA graduates should use email or SMS-based OTPs, ensure token expiration, and encrypt communication via HTTPS. Implementing device recognition and multi-factor authentication (MFA) provides added security. Preventing token reuse and monitoring login attempts mitigate risks of unauthorized access.

177. Discuss how ethical personalization can enhance user experience in news aggregator platforms.
Answer: Personalization tailors content but must avoid creating filter bubbles. MCA graduates should allow users to control personalization settings, provide diverse content exposure, and use algorithms transparently. Ethical personalization ensures user autonomy and prevents bias reinforcement in news consumption.

178. Analyze how to implement scalable video conferencing features in web applications.
Answer: Video conferencing requires low latency and high scalability. MCA graduates should use WebRTC for peer-to-peer communication, implement TURN servers for NAT traversal, and employ SFUs (Selective Forwarding Units) for multi-party calls. Load balancing and cloud-based infrastructure ensure reliable performance under high user loads.

179. Explain how to secure browser local storage in financial web applications.
Answer: Local storage is vulnerable to XSS attacks and should not hold sensitive data. MCA graduates should encrypt non-sensitive data if used, apply strict Content Security Policies (CSP), and use HTTP-only cookies for authentication tokens to prevent unauthorized access.

180. Discuss how to optimize web forms for usability and accessibility in government portals.
Answer: Usable and accessible forms ensure inclusivity. MCA graduates should use semantic HTML, proper labeling, and ARIA attributes for screen readers. Providing inline error validation, keyboard navigation, and clear instructions enhances accessibility for all users, including those with disabilities.

181. Explain how serverless architecture benefits web developers in building scalable apps.
Answer: Serverless computing abstracts infrastructure management, allowing developers to focus on code. MCA graduates should use platforms like AWS Lambda for event-driven tasks and auto-scaling. Serverless architecture reduces operational overhead and is cost-effective for workloads with unpredictable traffic.

182. Analyze the ethical implications of tracking user behavior in educational web apps.
Answer: Tracking can help tailor learning experiences but raises privacy concerns. MCA graduates should anonymize data, provide opt-out options, and disclose data usage policies to users. Balancing insights with ethical practices fosters trust among students and educators.

183. Discuss how to secure API gateways in microservices-based web applications.
Answer: API gateways handle sensitive traffic and require robust security. MCA graduates should implement authentication (OAuth/JWT), rate limiting, and traffic monitoring. Using HTTPS and validating incoming data at the gateway level reduces exposure to attacks across microservices.

184. Explain how to design a real-time collaborative whiteboard web application.
Answer: Real-time collaboration requires low-latency updates and conflict resolution. MCA graduates should use WebSockets for bi-directional communication and data structures like CRDTs to merge simultaneous changes. Scalable backend storage ensures persistence and reliability.

185. Discuss how ethical AI usage in recommendation engines impacts user trust.
Answer: AI-driven recommendations must avoid bias and manipulation. MCA graduates should ensure fairness in algorithms, provide transparency about how recommendations are generated, and allow users to customize preferences to maintain ethical standards.

186. Explain how to implement secure content delivery for premium video streaming services.
Answer: Premium streaming services require DRM (Digital Rights Management) to protect content. MCA graduates should use encrypted streaming protocols (e.g., HLS with AES encryption) and issue short-lived signed URLs to prevent unauthorized sharing or downloads.

187. Analyze how web accessibility audits improve user inclusivity in retail websites.
Answer: Accessibility audits identify barriers for users with disabilities. MCA graduates should use tools like Lighthouse and manual testing to ensure compliance with WCAG guidelines. Enhancing color contrast, providing keyboard support, and adding alt text improve inclusivity and expand the customer base.

188. Discuss how to prevent API abuse in public-facing web platforms.
Answer: Public APIs are prone to abuse through excessive requests or malicious payloads. MCA graduates should implement rate limiting, API keys, IP whitelisting, and request validation. Logging and anomaly detection help identify unusual patterns for proactive defense.

189. Explain how to use Content Delivery Networks (CDNs) to secure static web assets.
Answer: CDNs cache static assets globally and provide security features. MCA graduates should enable SSL/TLS on CDNs, use signed URLs for access control, and activate WAFs (Web Application Firewalls) at the edge to block malicious traffic before it reaches the origin server.

190. Discuss how ethical considerations shape UX design in financial budgeting apps.
Answer: Budgeting apps deal with sensitive financial data and user emotions. MCA graduates should avoid manipulative nudges towards overspending and ensure transparency in displaying financial insights. Ethical design prioritizes user well-being and trust.

191. Explain how to implement rate limiting on authentication APIs to prevent brute-force attacks.
Answer: Rate limiting restricts repeated failed login attempts. MCA graduates should enforce thresholds (e.g., 5 attempts per minute per IP), introduce exponential backoff delays, and implement CAPTCHA challenges to block automated bots. Logging failed attempts aids in detecting suspicious activity.

192. Analyze how server-side rendering (SSR) improves SEO in e-commerce Single Page Applications (SPAs).
Answer: SPAs load content dynamically, which search engines may not index effectively. MCA graduates should implement SSR frameworks like Next.js to serve pre-rendered HTML for better SEO and faster initial page loads, benefiting e-commerce platforms where discoverability drives revenue.

193. Discuss how to secure cloud databases used in web applications.
Answer: Cloud databases require stringent access controls. MCA graduates should enforce encrypted connections (SSL), use firewall rules to limit IP access, and enable automatic backups. Role-based permissions ensure only authorized users access sensitive data.

194. Explain how to design an API for IoT devices with low processing power and memory.
Answer: IoT APIs must be lightweight. MCA graduates should use compact data formats (e.g., Protocol Buffers), minimize request overhead, and design stateless endpoints to reduce memory usage. Secure communication via TLS ensures data integrity.

195. Discuss how ethical considerations guide targeted marketing in health-related web apps.
Answer: Health apps collect highly sensitive data. MCA graduates should ensure targeted marketing is opt-in, avoid exploiting vulnerabilities, and maintain user anonymity in analytics to align with ethical and legal standards like HIPAA.

196. Explain how to prevent CSRF attacks in REST APIs used by SPAs.
Answer: CSRF protection involves using anti-CSRF tokens or implementing SameSite cookie attributes. MCA graduates should validate request origins and ensure sensitive actions require explicit user confirmation. These measures prevent attackers from forging authenticated requests.

197. Analyze how web developers can implement secure session expiration strategies.
Answer: Sessions should expire after inactivity or a maximum lifespan. MCA graduates should implement sliding expiration, clear tokens on logout, and detect simultaneous sessions to prevent hijacking. Short-lived JWTs with refresh tokens maintain security in token-based systems.

198. Discuss how to design an inclusive registration form for a global audience.
Answer: Global registration forms must account for diverse cultural contexts. MCA graduates should support multiple languages, allow flexible name fields, and avoid assumptions about gender or phone number formats. Accessibility considerations like keyboard navigation ensure usability for all users.

199. Explain how to secure real-time notifications in banking web apps.
Answer: Real-time notifications should transmit over encrypted WebSocket (WSS) connections. MCA graduates should authenticate clients, validate payloads, and use tokens with short lifetimes. Ensuring sensitive data is never sent in plain text maintains security.

200. Discuss how ethical dark patterns affect user trust in subscription-based platforms.
Answer: Dark patterns like hidden fees or hard-to-find cancel options erode trust. MCA graduates should design transparent flows, provide clear opt-out choices, and prioritize user autonomy to foster long-term customer relationships.

9 789369 728213

Printed at Repro India Ltd.